My Year
as
Manx Bard

Sara Goodwins

Loaghtan Books
Caardee, Dreemskerry Hill
Maughold
Isle of Man
IM7 1BE

Published by Loaghtan Books

First published: October 2018

Copyright © Sara Goodwins 2018

Typesetting and origination by:
Loaghtan Books

Printed and bound by:
Latimer Trend

Website: www.loaghtanbooks.com

ISBN: 978-1-908060-22-8

Photographic copyright
© George Hobbs 2018
unless otherwise indicated

All rights reserved. No part of this publication may be reproduced, stored on a retrieval system or transmitted in any form or by any means without prior permission of the publishers.

For my husband George Hobbs,
who for the year called himself the Bard Consort
and our car the Bardmobile.
He doesn't much like poetry,
but without his help and support,
none of this would have happened.
A very nice man.

Front cover: The Manx Bardic robes on Port Cornaa beach

Rear cover: The author at Cashtal-yn-Ard

Title page: The Manx Bard's hat

Contents page: Details of the Manx Bardic robes and hat

CONTENTS

	Foreword	4
1	What is a Bard?	5
2	Applying to be Manx Bard	13
3	Aftermath	22
4	Poems in the paper	27
5	Duties and appearances	52
6	Highlights	69
7	Particular poems	82
8	A little bit about poetry	87
9	Me	93

HIS EXCELLENCY SIR RICHARD GOZNEY KCMG CVO

GOVERNMENT HOUSE
ISLE OF MAN
IM3 1RR

I am glad, and honoured, to be asked by Sara Goodwins, the Manx Bard for 2017-18, to preface her book about her eventful year.

Sara guides a fluent pen with ease, or gives us every appearance of ease. Her prose style will delight those who pick up this book and prompt many smiles. It reads well. Her poems are all revealing and contrast in style as well as content. Readers will choose their favourites. Mine are 'Legends or Leg-ends' which brings a fresh look to an old story, and 'After Work' which caricatures, somewhat, how the 'retired' swap a predictable working day for a helter-skelter of new, unfamiliar options. To one who was 'retired' for a few years in my early 60s it struck a chord.

I warmly commend Sara Goodwins' 'My Year as Manx Bard'.

- *Sir Richard Gozney KCMG CVO - Lieutenant Governor of the Isle of Man*
  September 2018

CHAPTER 1

WHAT IS A BARD?

Bards are very old. Not as individuals of course, but as an important part of the community. When Celts were living in round houses, when Christianity was the new religion and most rulers relied on druids as lawgivers, when people lived in small communities, built their own houses, made their own clothes and grew their own food, bards travelled from place to place, usually on foot, bringing news, entertainment and gossip in almost equal measure.

Bards were probably invented in the sixth century, and probably in Ireland. Being a Celtic country, the idea soon spread to the rest of the Celtic world – Wales, Scotland, Cornwall, Brittany and, of course the Isle of Man. In fact there's a thought that the French troubadours, who flourished from the eleventh to thirteenth centuries, actually developed from the Breton bards. The Celts got there first and the French pinched the idea! And there were female Bards as well as male. The Celtic world allowed its women far more freedom than most other cultures of the time.

Laxey Old Road. Once the main road into Laxey

Bards were not just entertainers, telling stories and making people laugh however. Much of the Celtic world – Ireland is the exception – had what is called an 'oral tradition', which means that history and cultural traditions are remembered rather than written down. The ancient Greeks did this, as did many of the Scandinavian countries and also Native Americans. An oral tradition is still important for many nomadic communities, particularly among the Kalahari bushmen of South Africa, and the horsemen of Mongolia. It makes sense. If you're a modern hunter-gatherer, moving around and living in a tent, then you can't carry a library around with you.

Some Bards found a rich household and stayed more or less in one place, 'paying' for their board and lodging by composing poems in praise of their patron and satires criticising his enemies. Most Bards, however, travelled from place to place and it was considered a great honour to have one staying under your roof. A Bard staying with you would turn your house into a temporary theatre, and all your neighbours would expect to be invited to listen to the Bard's stories. It would probably cost you quite a lot in beer!

**WRITTEN BY CANDLELIGHT
DURING A POWER CUT**

They called the hurricane 'Ophelia':
Sweet maid from Hamlet. As though such a name
Made elemental forces touchy-feelier.
We do not learn. We can't constrain or tame
Such power. The wisest of us hope
To work with wind and weather where it can
Make a difference, otherwise learn to cope
With its excesses. No matter how we plan
Even a small storm can find devouring
Mankind's careful structures only too easy;
All our vaunted strength reduced to cowering
If the wind grows too much more than breezy.

And so we sit, tablet, laptop, iPad
Stilled. Rain the only noise, our light the fire.
Just so, our forebears sat in caves, or, nomad,
Crouched in skin shelters to keep them drier.
They too might have named their storms, placating
Raging spirits who screamed in madness, hurled
Lightning, rocks, uprooted trees, berating
Puny men who thought they ruled the world.

Millennia have passed, yet still the storms
Still us. Untamed and flailing, rage and blow.
Ophelia went mad, a prey to brainstorms:
Perhaps the name's more fitting than we know.

The local community would have sat enthralled on the earth floor in your thatched hut, the only light the fire, listening to someone who had travelled to places they could only dream about. I was reminded of simpler times when the island was battered by hurricane Ophelia, and I wrote *Written by Candlelight during a Power Cut*. The title is something of a give away.

Incidentally, it's interesting how poetry develops, or I find it so. In *Written by Candlelight...* I was stuck for a word in the last line. I had 'accurate', as in 'perhaps the name's more accurate than we know'. It wasn't a good word. 'Accurate' has three syllables instead of two and the stress is in the wrong place, so I sent the poem to a friend, also a poet, and asked what she thought. She wondered why I hadn't used the word 'fitting', which was so totally right, I changed it immediately. (She's a genius!) I did however warn her that I'd make sure that everyone knew it was her idea. So, please note: the word 'fitting' is copyright Frances Chambers who lives in Yorkshire.

Bard's robes are traditionally light blue. The colour reflects the colour of the sky, which for the Celtic community would have been a symbol of peace. Blue is a colour which is difficult and expensive to obtain using traditional or natural dyes. In Celtic countries, blue dye would have been obtained from the leaves of woad or, at a pinch, from cornflowers. Woad seeks out and invades cultivated land, so those growing food crops would not have appreciated its presence. On the other hand, its use in dyes made it valuable and woad balls were occasionally used as trading tokens or as a rudimentary currency.

Because blue was so uncommon, anyone wearing it would have immediately been marked out as in some way set apart. Someone of high social class might wear blue because of their rank, a Bard would wear blue because of their calling.

The Manx Bard's robes were designed and made by Linda Davies, who had never made anything like them before. I think she's done a superb job.

Because they travelled about a lot and usually on foot, the Bardic staff was originally partly a walking stick and partly a quarterstaff, i.e. a means of defence. We've all seen films of Robin Hood whirling a long pole to fight off his enemies; the Bardic staff was used for the same sort of swashbuckling. It was considered very bad luck to harm a Bard – in an oral tradition it would be a little like burning down a library – but, if you're an outlaw with a price on your head, living rough and likely to die a horrible death if you're caught, you probably wouldn't be too bothered about bad luck, so a Bard needed some means of defending themselves.

The robes are lovely, but it is actually the staff which gives the bard authority, like the swagger stick of army officers, or the church sidesmen's wand.

Today the staff is ceremonial, although it's very good for dealing with hecklers.

The Manx Bardic staff is mahogany, 64 inches long and was designed and made on the Isle of Man by Simon Capelan. The design at the top represents the all-seeing eye of Manannan, the island's traditional protector.

SONNET

LIFE'S MEASURE

What will my feet be like when I am old?
I see them, shapeless, in their battered shell
Of scuffed and moulting slippers. Flat brogues, well
Worn in, ease joints still aching yet enrolled
To service. Reckless youth craved glamour, bold
Shop window fittings which were strappy hell
To wear. Years more and worn out feet soon quell
Discomfort, peaceful in wool, defeating cold.

Five toes on each foot, meta and tarsal
Grouped, short of its measure, barely more than half:
Six hobbled inches, a useless parcel
Of painful bunions… Yet, provide a path
A destination, tiptoe, limp and stride,
And stillness only can their purpose hide.

One other thing I should perhaps clarify: bards were not druids! I was surprised to find that there is sometimes confusion about this. A Bard actually cannot also be a druid, or at least not at the same time; historically the two roles are interdependent but distinct. It's rather like the Speaker of the Manx House of Keys, can never also be the island's Lieutenant Governor.

In history druids were a mix of lawgiver and leader with a dash of religion thrown in. They weren't necessarily rulers, but something of an *eminence gris*, the powerful advisor at the ruler's right hand. A Bard, as we've seen, is nothing like that. Bards wandered about, druids stayed in their community; bards told stories, druids passed laws; bards entertained, druids… didn't.

Traditionally bards were taught the various verse forms and studied how to write and play music on various instruments. Prospective bards also learned how to find a patron and, once found, how to please them through poetry. Many would be taught by an older Bard as a sort of apprentice, but there are suggestions that Wales and possibly Ireland had some sort of formal Bard school. Many Bards, once they took up their calling, would choose a Bardic name, and this persists today. My Bardic name, for example, is *Ta cairys cosney*, which means 'righteousness prevails', or, if you prefer, 'good wins'. The biggest congregation of bards today is in Wales with the *Eisteddfodau*, although Cornwall seems to be catching up fast with its *Gorsedhau*.

The modern invention of Manx Bard was the brainchild of Bridget Carter, who approached Culture Vannin for support. Culture Vannin is the trading name of the Manx Heritage Foundation and supports the Manx Bard as a way of encouraging

CELTIC ARTWORK

Original inhabitants of Mann,
Their balanced knotwork marked the artisan:
Flowing lines wove ornament round shields,
Torques, helmets; known on battlefields
Through Europe. Swirling chains, mysterious,
Link clan to clan with power imperious.

Blond Vikings came; their newer power invaded
Retreating to the shadows, dark Celts faded.
Square halls replaced round houses – new upstarts.
Celts left no written record, but their arts
Speak for them. Fluid and inscrutable,
Their dazzling prowess indisputable.

Once a symbol of a chieftain's might,
These artefacts remain to dazzle sight.
They, excavated spoils from mausoleums,
Now entertain the tourists in museums.

This page: the Bardic chair, designed and made by Simon Capelan and Graham Hall Opposite page: Druidale

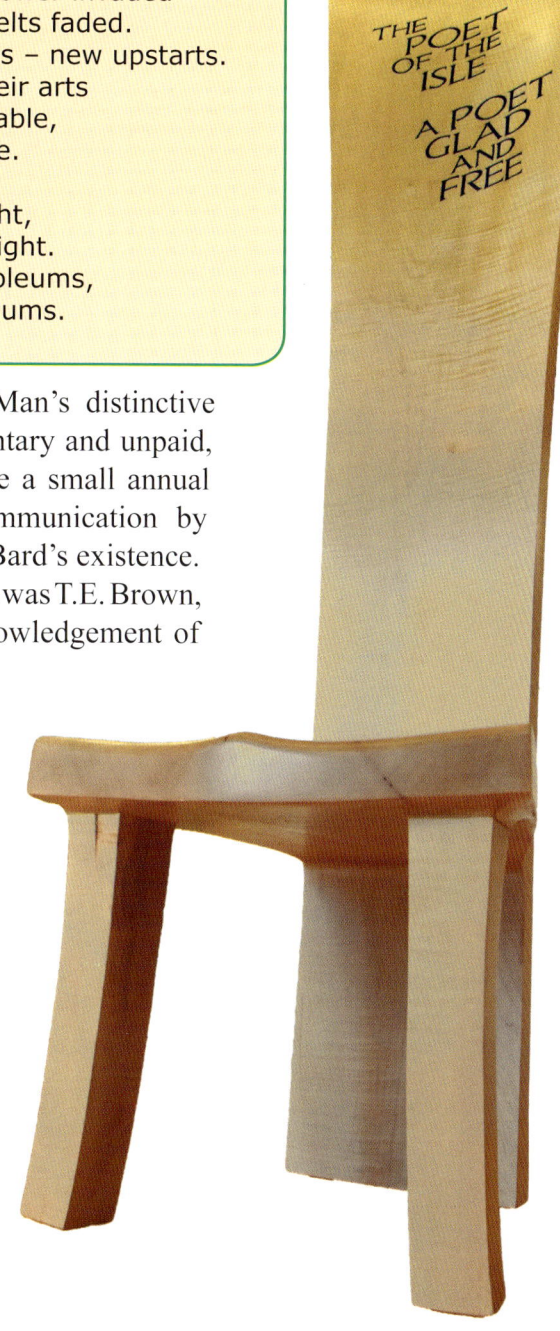

local poets to promote the Isle of Man's distinctive and unique culture. The post is voluntary and unpaid, although Culture Vannin does provide a small annual stipend to cover expenses, and communication by poetry is still the main reason for the Bard's existence.

The first Manx Bard of modern times was T.E. Brown, appointed posthumously and in acknowledgement of the fact that he was probably the best-known of the Manx poets. A Victorian teacher and poet he died in 1897. Stacey Astill (see page 18) is the second Manx Bard, one of whose poems can be seen on the window of Noble's library. The third Manx Bard is John 'Dog' Callister (see page 28), a well-known Manx poet and craftsman. I'm the fourth and Annie Kissack is the fifth.

Although each year a new Bard is appointed, becoming Bard is a lifetime appointment.

BORN TO BE BARD

'I'm fourth Manx Bard you know,' 'Oh yes?
That must be easy – let me guess;
You merely have to write some rhymes,
Old-fashioned stuff for modern times.
I'd find the duties quite a curse,
But you can go from Bard to Verse.'

Still chuckling he walked away.
Through gritted teeth I tried to say:
'You're not the first to make that joke,
Don't think it is a masterstroke.'
Quips and puns – I've heard them all,
Their telling lacks a protocol.

Some people mention to me, smugly:
'The Good, the Bard, and then the Ugly –
Which are you?' I say, 'such platitude
Creates a thoroughly Bard Attitude.'
Ignoring hints they merely say
I must be having a Bard Day.

With words like that I cannot win
So think I might as well join in.

My poems may be Good or Bard,
Hated or treated with regard,
Be Bard News or thought five
    starred,
Easy to understand or hard,
But still I am no window
    shard:
You can't see through:
    I'm No Holes Bard.

My term of office has now ended, but I shall always be the fourth Manx Bard. The current Bard tends to be viewed as the 'senior' Bard for their year in office, and, consequently, tends to be busier than the other Bards. However all the Bards make public appearances, either through invitation or by standing in for each other.

This page:
Statue of T.E. Brown, the first Manx Bard. It stands on the corner of Bucks Road and Circular Road in Douglas
Opposite page:
Cashtal-yn-Ard

CHAPTER 2

APPLYING TO BE MANX BARD

Different Celtic nations have different rules for appointing Bards. In Cornwall, for example, the title of Bard, can be awarded to more than one individual per year, but is awarded only to those who have studied the Cornish language and music, have worked to preserve the Cornish culture and heritage, and who have been proposed, without their knowledge, by an existing Bard. In the Isle of Man, when I applied, only one Bard is appointed per year, after a straight competition. A Bard is a lifetime appointment, so previous and current bards don't apply again and prospective Bards compete against each other.

> Why be Manx Bard? – People often ask that. My usual reply Is that I like the hat...

Any poet can apply, they need only to be over eighteen and permanent residents of the Isle of Man for their year in office. Rather to my surprise there was no requirement for Bards to be Manx speakers or even to learn the language. Those putting themselves forward for consideration had to supply up to three poems, plus a 500-word proposal setting out what they intended to do in their bardic year. I submitted two poems about Manx subjects and one which was more general. My first choice was *Legends or Leg-ends?* (see next page) which is about as Manx as anything I've written could be.

13

LEGENDS OR LEG-ENDS?

The pub was warm and cosy, many locals gathered round
To discuss their nationality and problems they had found:
'When visiting', cried one of them, 'folk think that I'm a Scot'
'Or English', said another, 'in fact everything I'm not.'
They all agreed but could not think how these mistakes to quash,
While a tabby cat sat by the fire and gave his paws a wash.
His name was Captain Tripod and he was an old Manx cat.
Some years before he'd lost a leg in battle with a rat.
He'd earned his bed beside the fire and, snoozing in his place,
Was still an able mouser and well worthy of his race.
A stranger listened to the talk, he was old and closely cloaked
Despite protective clothing his hair and beard were soaked.
They welcomed him beside the fire, he gave a nod of thanks,
And said: 'you need a symbol to let people know you're Manx.'
He pointed to his leggings, and the stool on which he sat
The golden firelight, blood-red wine, and even to the cat.
'Three legs in armour's what you need, united, all for one.
Put them against a bright red flag and shape them like the sun.
For motto let it state the Manx are tough and love their land:
"No matter what you do to me you know that I shall stand"'
Each looked at each and nodded; they were pleased and none said nay,
And while they were agreeing old Manannan slipped away.

And that's why Mann has got three legs, joined, balanced on their toes:
They represent the island…. or so the story goes.

Although I was and am very pleased with the poem, it does cause the occasional problem. A UK audience would think nothing of the inclusion of the R.A.T. word, but it's one that the Manx would never pronounce. On island the rodent is always called a longtail and using the three-letter name is simply not done. Even spelling it out as above is only just acceptable. Whenever I read that poem to a Manx audience I have to remember to substitute, and to hope that the audience will understand what the rhyme is supposed to be. (The only rhyme I've been able to think of for 'longtail' is 'strong ale', which would go with the pub setting, I suppose...)

My second poem was a sonnet (see page 92 for more about sonnets) *Return of the Hero*, and was the least Manx poem of the three. Hindsight is a wonderful thing, but I think I would have been wiser to have chosen something easier to read aloud.

Jurby church and war memorial

SONNET

RETURN OF THE HERO

Kill. They said. Commanded hands stole breath.
In noise young men let blood, were forced to yield.
Meanwhile in cold stone churches quiet they kneeled
Who had condemned them to their task of death:
Once done with pride they claimed them for their faith.
Modest warriors, comfortless, revealed
Trinkets for trophies. All else shame concealed
Snared, compared to their enemies' wraith.

Veiled hero, scarred by chance and choice
Shrunken in anguish cried to stranger friend:
'I cannot give again my strength my voice
To that I was. They still control my end.
Stunted, I cannot hide in form so far
From mine. My task is yet to mend. Or mar.'

Candidates considered suitable for consideration for the post of Manx Bard were short listed and then invited for interview by a panel made up of members of the Bard committee and those with influence in Manx arts and culture. Six people interviewed me, including Bridget Carter, chair of the Bard committee, and Stacey Astill, the first living bard of modern times.

At the interview I was asked what I would do as Bard were I to be appointed, questioned about my knowledge of Manx life and culture and asked to read my

THE HORSE'S REPLY

'Promenade' is French for 'walkway'
Four legs or two unsaid,
But, impatient, hurried, stressed, alone
You prefer your car instead.

What happened to Manx friendliness?
What price is *traa dy liooar*?
After fourteen decades service
Don't you want me anymore?

What about your children's children?
And the tourists who have fun?
Will they be pleased you stopped the trams?
Will they still want to come?

You complain I slow the traffic.
But the problem's all the cars –
And visitors who ride with me
Spend cash in shops and bars.

If you make the horses homeless
Tourists may stay away,
As tram-less, boring, car-filled towns
They can get in the UK.

three poems aloud. I also expressed my surprise that Manx was not a requirement, and was quite open about the fact that I did not speak the language – of which more anon (see page 85).

> **BARDIC BOTHERINGS**
>
> I need to write a poem
> If I want to be Manx Bard
> To fill the application form;
> It shouldn't be too hard.
>
> But what should be the topic?
> Must be good if I'm to pass:
> Global Warming's stiff and serious
> Good scope and *gravitas*.
>
> Political Incorrectness
> I'd have great fun deploring
> But perhaps they'll fidget, yawn and think
> It's passé, dull and boring.
>
> Something Manx should be the thing –
> Perhaps a 'Brown' memorial?
> But I mustn't seem too limited
> When the post's ambassadorial.
>
> Could I write to rival Shakespeare
> The most famous Bard of all?:
> 'What light through yonder window breaks'...
> ... Er... Best start with something small.
>
> I need to write a poem
> If Manx Bard I want to be
> Perhaps it's this? I've done it!
> This is my third of three!

My third poem was, originally, to be about the Douglas Bay Tramway, or 'the horse trams' as they're more usually known. In 2016, in their 140th year, they were threatened with closure. (Madness!) I was so appalled that I wrote *The Horse's Reply* (see previous page) and intended that to be my third poem for bardic application purposes.

In fact the application was nearly scuppered – accidentally – by the Bard of the time. Three days before I was due to submit my entry, John 'Dog' Callister, the third Manx Bard (see page 28), had a poem in the local paper about... the horse trams. Not wanting to appear as though I were copying his idea, I had hurriedly to find – or write – something else. I came up with *Bardic Botherings*.

Interview over I escaped to let other poets be grilled. None of us would know who the successful candidate was until the following day when the new Bard was to be inaugurated.

Stacey Astill, second Manx Bard, performing at the 2017 Bardic inauguration

What's the moos? 2017 Bardic inauguration. Photograph © Hannah Carter

I don't remember a great deal about the actual inauguration. The event was held in a barn on Moorhouse Farm just north of Port St Mary. Owner and farmer Paul Costain is a popular bass singer and, at the time of writing, two times winner of the prestigious Cleveland Medal at the Manx Music Festival (2016 and 2018). He's a good friend and supporter of the Bard committee and his barn made a useful, if unusual, concert hall. At one stage a curious cow poked its head through a gap in the wall, decided that these odd humans were not interfering with bovine concerns, were, furthermore, inedible, and went away again.

The guests were numerous and exalted and George and I spent a happy time celebrity spotting. ('Oh gosh, there's the Lieutenant Governor!' 'That's Pullyman; I like his poems.' 'Why is the Speaker wearing wellies?' 'Isn't that the President of Tynwald; he looks different without his formal wig?'... and so on.)

Entertainment was provided by various guests reading some of the work of the major Manx poets, while the Bards read some of their own. Each performer had been given a time slot and it all worked well, apart from one gentleman who overran horrendously and seemed not to notice that his audience was growing bored, fidgeting and, in some cases, wandering away. Highlights of the proceedings included regular punctuation by the whistles of steam trains as they crossed the level crossing at Mount Gawne Road. The line runs directly behind the barn and, had we had a mind to, we could have shaken hands with the passengers.

Paul Costain singing with Caarjyn Cooidjagh

There was also music by the Manx Gaelic Choir *Caarjyn Cooidjagh* (which means 'friends together'), Paul Costain, and Manx harpist Mera Royle. It was a splendid and thoroughly enjoyable programme.

Not being Manx – I'm what the island knows as a 'comeover' – I was quite sure that they wouldn't give such a prestigious post to me, so was fairly relaxed as George and I sat at the back of the straw-bale seating to be out of the way for The Announcement. The job fell to Juan Watterson, Speaker of the House of Keys and, appropriately, Member of the House of Keys for Rushen, the sheading into which Moorhouse Farms falls. Local boy made good.

Mr Speaker produced The Envelope, opened it and, with a commendably short speech read out... my name. My. Name.

I sat there with my mouth open. George, who always has more presence of mind than me, dug me in the ribs and hissed, 'it's you, get up, Get Up, they want you out at the front, Get UP!'.

After that it's all a bit of a blur. I tripped over the handle of my camera bag and stumbled out, trampling on other people's possessions, bags, feet as I tried to extricate myself from the back row (sorry, **sorry,** *sorry*). I think I may have inadvertently clouted the Lieutenant Governor with my swinging coat – sorry again – and finally clambered to the front where the Bard committee shoehorned me into the robes. If you look at pictures of me I look either drunk (I wasn't) or as though I'd been hit with a spade (I hadn't been). Then they asked me to read one of my poems and –

panic! – I hadn't brought anything with me! Fortunately Hazel Teare, one of the interview panel, took pity on my idiocy and pushed her copy of my poem into my shaking hands (thank you Hazel!). It was

> **THANK YOU**
>
> Thank you. It's so small a word
> To use it now seems quite absurd –
> Inadequate, self conscious, trite
> Acknowledgement of that which might
> Seem honouring beyond my due
> The skills of which I have such few.
>
> But now – Manx Bard – at your behest
> I thank you. I will do my best

blessedly familiar and I read *Legends or Legends?* (see page 14). I was so confubulated, however, that I actually *said* the wretched R.A.T. word, instead of substituting 'longtail' as I usually do, and promptly upset a large part of the audience. Sorry once more.

About the only thing I got right is thanks to my husband. Before the event, he suggested that I put together a short poem of thanks in the very unlikely circumstance that I was appointed. Taking his advice, I did. Despite the fog in the brain, I even managed to remember it. George, you're a star.

21

CHAPTER 3

AFTERMATH

The first week after being appointed Bard passed in a flurry of media activity. Naively I was taken by surprise at the interest the Manx media showed in the new Bard, and was invited to appear on a number of radio programmes or contribute to newspapers and journals. The Isle of Man has no television station, apart from manx.net/tv, so I was spared too much camera work. This was all to the good; I have an excellent face for radio.

The Manx Bard is responsible for deciding what they do during their bardic year and, early on, I'd taken the decision to write a new poem every time I was invited somewhere in my official capacity. As I had no idea how busy I'd be I was aware that I could be setting myself the task of writing quite a lot of poetry, but I saw that as part of the Bard's job. Consequently the first week saw me temporarily ditching the day job – I'm self employed so this was at least

LIVE INTERVIEW

A Spartan room, yet brightly lit,
Two chairs and the transmitting kit.

Why nervous? Just a microphone
A chat with someone on their own.

But broadcast waves take words afar
To people listening in their car,
Fathers ironing, mothers cooking,
Children on their mobiles looking
Up to see who's speaking,
Then resuming Facebook tweaking.
People shopping, husbands, wives –
My voice a background to their lives.

The moment passes fleetingly;
I speak to those I'll never see.

Meanings differ: 'Live on Air'
Is not the same as life out there.

possible – and either writing poetry or meeting various media personalities for live or recorded interviews.

Live Interview was the poem I wrote when invited to appear (can one 'appear' on radio?) on *Women Today* presented by Beth Espey and Christy DeHaven. I rather like the poem. It was one of those rare times when the words flowed very easily. Mostly I find writing poetry extremely hard

... FOR MANDATE INTERVIEW

If you want to know what's going on
Try Mandate

Tune in to airways flowing on
To Mandate

News from the nation's station
Giving out Manx information
Interspersed with conversation
That's Mandate

For the gossip and the skeet
And the story from your street
You will get a ringside seat
From Mandate

Learn about the famous names
Find out all the fun and games
Compèred by Davis, James
On Mandate

SONNET

NOT SURE

Opinions are important, so we think.
Yet why? We are no oracles to try
To forecast, solve or otherwise to cry
Off fate, turning back disaster from the brink.
No. Mostly we go with the flow, tipping the wink
To ignorance, making our best guess. Why
Then expect the certainty which does not lie
Within ourselves, in others? There is no link.

We are suspicious of too much assertion,
Rightly distrusting those opinionated
Fools who, doubt free, make our tempers worsen
Escalating conflict. Only weighted
Deliberation can help our knowledge grow.
'Til then, it's best to own that we don't know.

work – more perspiration than inspiration – but this poem almost wrote itself. I think it shows.

And, at the risk of sounding sycophantic, I was really impressed by the professionalism of all those who work in

View from the headland near Manx Radio

the media, but particularly by Beth and Christy. There are lots of jobs I couldn't do, but few where this is demonstrated with such professional ease. They manage to relax and chat during the advert breaks and then switch smoothly into professional presenting at less than a second's notice. No 'ums' and 'ers', no hesitation, no distracting nerves, all of which I was guilty of. Amazing. And very hard to do.

I also appeared very briefly on *Mandate*, presented at the time by James Davis. James had been with Manx Radio for fifteen years but left shortly after our chat; I trust the two events aren't related. From my point of view his leaving is a pity as, quite apart from the fact that he's a very nice chap, the poem is now out of date.

The only programme on which I appeared and for which I failed to write a poem was Bob Carswell's *Shiaght Laa*, which is a bilingual programme in both Manx and English. Not being a Manx speaker I wasn't able to do a bilingual poem and so thought it best not to write one in English alone. Sorry Bob. I regretted that decision later, but managed to correct it when I appeared on *Shiaght Laa* again at the end of my tenure to talk about my Bardic year. For those who don't know *bannaght lhiu* means 'farewell'.

I was also stood up! Someone (I'll mention no names) from the magazine *Spotlight* arranged to meet me at the Noa Bakehouse in Douglas. The Manx Grand Prix aka Festival of Motorcycling was on at the time, which meant that travelling by road wasn't easy so I decided to catch the Manx Electric Railway to Douglas. (The MER's more fun anyway.) Arriving at Derby Castle I hopped onto a horse tram. I arrived in good time, bought myself a coffee and settled down to wait. I waited. And I waited. And I waited some more. I don't own a mobile phone – there are a few of us dinosaurs left – but the Bakehouse people knew for whom I was waiting and very kindly rang them. They were in Port Erin! They'd forgotten!! Never mind. Their poem was a sonnet, called, appropriately *Spotlight*.

FOR SHIAGHT LAA

Bob Carswell interviewed me for
Shiaght Laa when I began
But I didn't speak the language
Native to the Isle of Man.

As Manx Bard I felt I ought to write
Bilingually, and fretted,
So I couldn't write Bob any verse
A thing I've long regretted.

Throughout my year as current Bard
I've felt my lack of Manx:
I tried to learn but found it hard
To join the adepts' ranks.

But I couldn't bring the curtain down,
Now that my time is through,
Without at least attempting
Something Manx, so... *bannaght lhiu*.

SONNET

SPOTLIGHT

The spotlight shines on nobody for long –
It's not designed so. An accent merely
To point the temporary showman; clearly
We are all part of the same strong
Play of life. Too much star-billing would be wrong.
Scene done, we step into shadow, sincerely
Saddened yet relieved. We are not really
Meant to be so much apart; we all belong.

But while the bright lights last
Speculative eyes see, gaze, look and stare
From darkness, point the contrast
Pinning the hapless subject lighted there.
Our difference is our risk
The spotlight, cage and freedom in a disk.

CHAPTER 4

POEMS IN THE PAPER

One of the duties of the Manx Bard is to provide a monthly poem for the *Island Life* section of *The Manx Independent* newspaper. The tradition, if it's not too young to be called such, was started by John 'Dog' Callister, continued with me and, at the time of writing, has been taken over by Annie Kissack.

The Bard provides not only a poem, but a short piece of text to explain how and why they came to write it. I tried make my twelve poems seasonal, or at least to link them with what was happening on the island at the time. The paper included not only the poem and its accompanying text, but also a photograph which helped illustrate both. Being married to a photographer we tried to supply *Island Life* with a complete package as it were, although there were one or two occasions where the press photographers had a more appropriate library of images from which to choose.

I was very pleasantly surprised and touched to learn how many people read and thought about the poems which appeared in the newspaper. Occasionally people asked whether I could send them a particular poem which they had intended to keep but had forgotten to cut out. This chapter, therefore, is really the result of such requests for a permanent record.

Embroidered triquetra (right) and triskelion on the Manx Bardic robes

September

I was appointed fourth Manx Bard on Sunday 20 August 2017, so the first of my poems to appear in the *Manx Independent* did so on 14 September. It was usually required for the second Thursday of the month, although on at least one occasion the day changed which threw me into a flat spin for getting the copy in on time.

I thought a long time about what I should do for the first poem from the new Bard, particularly as I was taking over the Bard's role from someone as well known as John 'Dog' Callister (see photograph). I considered the Bard to be very much a celebration of all things Manx and, as I've said, I'm not Manx. No matter how much I like the island and love living here, I wasn't born here. (Very bad planning on the part of my parents I always feel.) I also, if I'm honest, wanted to avoid getting into any wrangle with those who might resent a comeover getting the job. I should say straight away, that no-one has expressed that opinion – at least not to me – and all have been very welcoming and supportive. But I didn't know they would be at the start.

So I thought that the first poem from the new Bard ought to 'set out the stall' so to speak. It ought to explain something about how I saw the Bard's role as an ambassador for Manx culture and heritage. I wanted the poem to acknowledge and thank the previous Bards whose mantle I'd inherited and whose work I was to continue. And I wanted to emphasise, if I could, that poetry is a way of saying things which are difficult to say any other way. I'm not sure that the new Bard's first poem for *Island Life* did all this, but here it is anyway.

STEPPING UP

John 'Dog' Callister's very hard
An act to follow as Manx Bard.
It's not his poetry alone
Which makes this craftsman so well known.

Curragh expert, gives guided walks
Complete with knowledgeable talks,
Cage for bumbees weaver, seer
Whose favourite building's Ramsey Pier.
At Milntown, willow dragonflies –
His making – leap into the skies:

A well-known Manxman. This I'm not
(Neither Manx nor man), but on the spot
To take the torch and carry on
Where others' feet before have gone.

The remit's wide; to celebrate
All things which make this island great.
It doesn't matter who is writing;
The work's important, for we're fighting
To keep alive – and this is key –
Manannan's Isle's identity.

That task is bigger than us all;
We work together or we fall.
'Comeover', 'English', and the rest
Is meaningless: I'll do my best.

October

The idea for the October poem was suggested by my husband. As I have mentioned, we live in Maughold and frequently see the Stena ships gliding past as they travel between Liverpool and Belfast. George's comment was that it was odd that they're so familiar and yet they never visit the island, but always pass by.

One thing which is particularly noticeable is that, for such large vessels, they can often pass unnoticed. The blue of the lower decks tends to blend with the sea and, if the day is overcast, they can barely be seen at all. On the other hand, if they're in sun the white paintwork of the upper decks gleams and they really stand out. What's really fascinating is watching them appear and disappear as they sail into

SHIPS THAT PASS

The isles across have ferries, Mann has boats –
A local soubriquet for that which floats –
But, isle to isle, the ferries ply their trade
From Liverpool to Belfast. Hove and fade
Into and out of view, like swans serene
In sun, their white remoteness clearly seen.
And, steaming in the darkness of the night
Manx lighthouses provide their guiding light.
So we're not unimportant where we lie…

What do they see when they go sailing by?
Small island cloaked in cloud twixt sky and sea,
Its mountains dipping to the plain, its people free.
Its rugged cliffs of rock, soft dunes of sand,
Fringing the greenness of this fertile land.
A brilliant jewel set in a cobalt sea.
When they go sailing by, what do they see?

Friendly strangers, as often are we all.
They see us, we them, and yet they never call…

and out of patches of sunlight. It's like magic. They can often be seen at night too when their lights float above the sea.

The ships usually pass several times a day, in each direction, and this got me thinking about what might be called the reverse effect; if we can see them, then they can see us. The island must be just as mysterious to people on the ships as they are to us, appearing occasionally in sunlight or hidden by Manannan's cloak.

The poem is written in rhyming couplets. Unusually the first verse break is between two rhymes. I rather liked that. It leaves the reader with impression of a tenuous link between the ships and the land they never visit. Or it might.

November

The beginning of November sees poppy sellers raising funds to support injured servicemen and women. It was obviously appropriate for this month's poem to reflect the sacrifice made in war, particularly as the publication date of the newspaper was so close to Remembrance Day itself.

I've always been impressed by the war memorial on Douglas promenade. It was designed by Ewart Crellin and is unusually tall and deceptively simple. It manages to be striking without being mawkish and I like the way it includes smaller conflicts as well as the two World Wars. I know of few other war memorials which honour the dead from the Korean War and the Aden Emergency. I also like where the memorial is sited, between the sea and the land, and near the Gaiety Theatre and Villa Marina, i.e. near where people congregate.

When I was growing up – I'm in my fifties – there were still many people who remembered fighting in the First World War. Within my lifetime the memories of both World Wars are beginning to fade, and there aren't now that many people left who remember even the Second World War. In some ways the Douglas war memorial seems to be almost a metaphor for how we remember those who died in war. Just as it is very easy to walk, cycle, drive or ride past and not look up at the Manxman standing at the top of the column, so, without prompting, we seldom remember the sacrifice of those who died. Our lives are so busy, that it's easy to forget that we have the life that we have, largely because men like him fought to protect it.

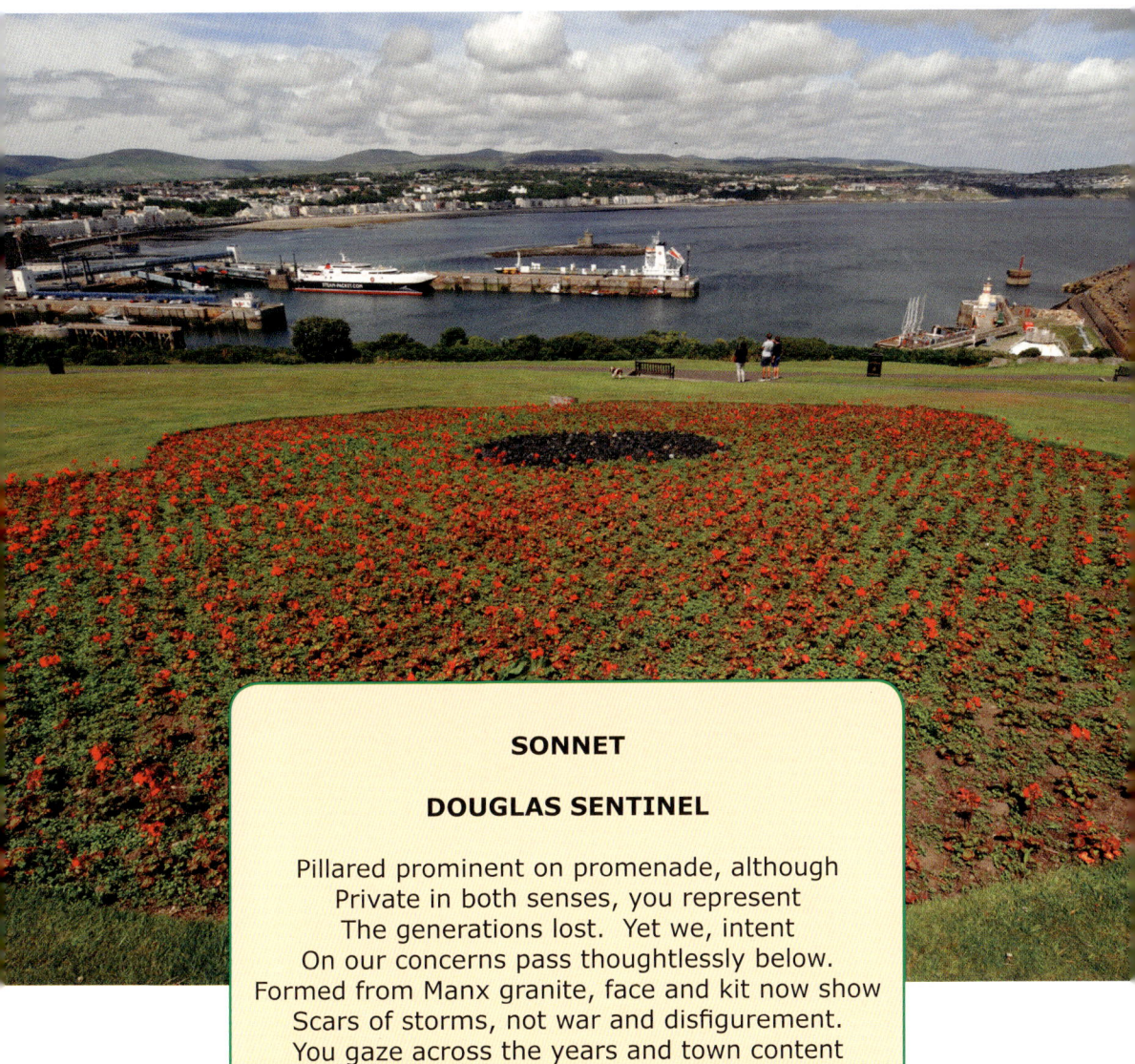

SONNET

DOUGLAS SENTINEL

Pillared prominent on promenade, although
Private in both senses, you represent
The generations lost. Yet we, intent
On our concerns pass thoughtlessly below.
Formed from Manx granite, face and kit now show
Scars of storms, not war and disfigurement.
You gaze across the years and town content
With rightful place and placing. Better so.

Familiar, yet remote, like those who died
Your figure is the fulcrum and the chain
Between the past and future, strand and tide
Balancing your losses with our gain.
Your pillar points a warning, and yet... and yet...
Do we still see its message? We must not forget.

December

It seemed obvious that the Bard's December poem should be linked with Christmas. That got me thinking about what Christmas means. I love Christmas. I love the lights and the carols, Christmas decorations and cards, Father Christmas visiting, and presents under the tree. But that's not really what Christmas is all about.

Christmas started with the birth of a baby. At this time of year the media often visit the maternity hospital to see which new babies share Jesus's birthday. Photos of proud parents with their tiny offspring often appear in the newspapers together with a little information about the new family.

That got me thinking about all the other families with new babies born at this time of the year, and also all those who have been born down the centuries. It also got me thinking about all the women who have acted as midwives for them. I've often wondered who helped Mary. Perhaps it was the innkeeper's wife.

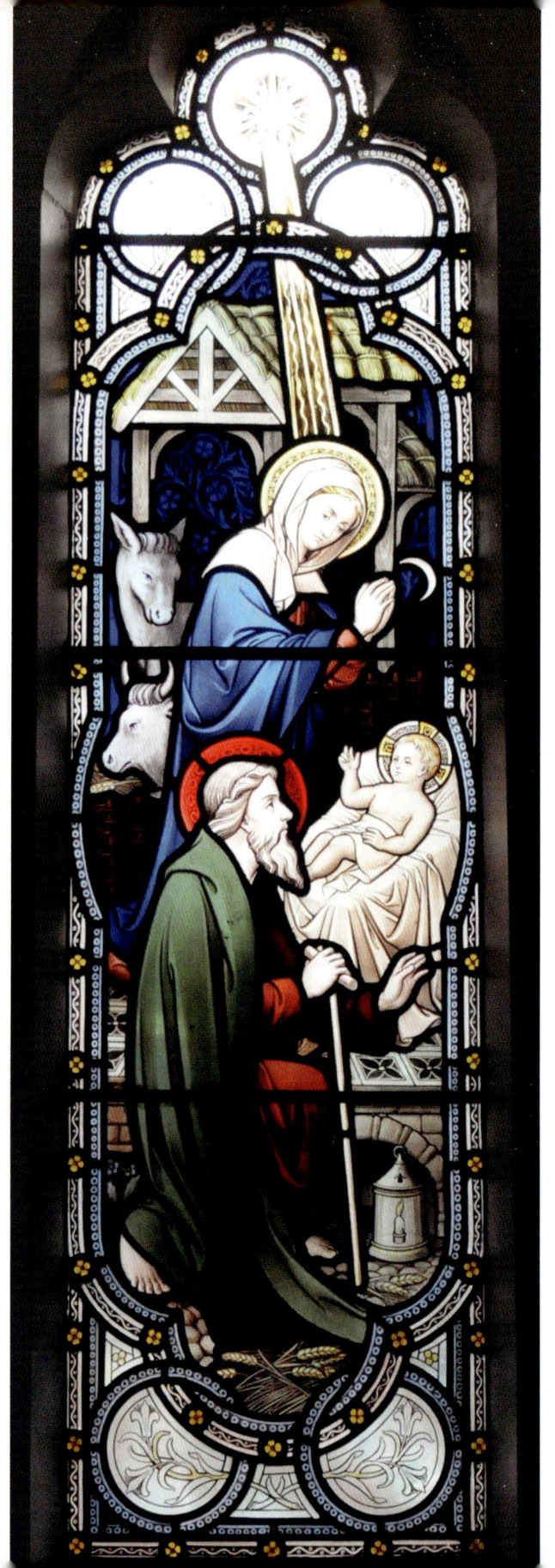

Then I thought about how, at the very beginning of their life, each baby is like a blank sheet of paper. The story of their life has to be written on it, and nobody knows how it will turn out. Heroes and villains all start the same way. Each baby is a miracle of new life and all new mothers think that their babies are special, of course they do.

The prophecies, the wise men, the angels all marked Jesus out to be special. Yet in one way he was very ordinary. He was just one of the babies born to doting mothers around that time.

I was concerned that the poem might shock readers. I hope it doesn't.

CHRISTMAS MIDWIFE

'Here you are, love, you've a son,
What d'you mean, "The Chosen One"?
All new Mums think that my dear;
Don't you fret now – he's right here.

'I love this age; no-one can tell
How they'll turn out. Oh, he'll do well.
You've not got much, but he's your love
As well as help from Him above.

'He might be champion of the poor,
Or try to change the Roman law.
Become a scholar, be well paid
Or follow in his father's trade.
So much can change the babes I've seen –
Be sinner, saint or in between.

'Don't look like you, though, nor his Dad;
That's normal for a little lad,
But, pardon me for saying this –
Your man's quite old; you sure he's his?
Oh, no offence! You wouldn't be
The first to stray, believe you me.

'I must away. Before I go
One thing I always like to know;
What name he'll carry through his time?
You'll call him... Judas! Well, that's fine!'

Stained glass windows of the Nativity (left) in St Paul's, Ramsey, and the crucifixion in St Bridget's, Bride

January

My father, who normally went to bed quite early, always insisted on staying up to see the New Year in. I continue the tradition and keep George, another one who prefers to retire early, up until after midnight. Poor man!

My Dad used to spend the evening before the start of a new year talking about what had happened in the year about to end. We used to remember the good times, and argue about what had gone wrong and how we should have done things differently. Hindsight is a wonderful thing! We also looked forward to what we might all be doing in the coming year. Many of our plans never came to anything, but we enjoyed making them.

Looking forward and looking back is where the name of the month comes from. January is named after Janus, the Roman god of gates and doorways, often depicted with two faces, one looking forward and one back.

So there I was with the topic of January's poem handed to me on a plate.

But then I thought, well, yes, all of that's all very well, but it's artificial isn't it? The whole New Year idea I mean. After all, it's just a number. The previous year was 2017 in the Isle of Man, 1379 in Burma, 5778 in Israel and 4714 or 4654 in China. And all the 'new years' don't start on the same day either.

SONNET

NEW YEAR

'The turning of the year'; a magic phrase
A magic time, of endings and beginnings,
Of looking back to see the old year's innings,
Of looking forward, measuring the days
Ready for challenges and seeking ways
To shape the new year. Underpinnings
Of hope reflected in the ringings
Of New Year bells mark more than holidays.

The first of January. We treat it
As a hinge between times past and now.
As though the year needs numbers to complete it.
Needless artifice. The ark of years will plough
Through temporal seas unhampered by our measures
And, indifferent, bring its cargo: pain or pleasures.

Opposite page: sundial in Patrick churchyard
This page: signpost on the Millennium Way where it crosses the B10 near Beinn-y-Phott

Time passes even if we don't number the seconds. The seasons carry on turning even if people are not there to label or count them. Things happen even if they are not planned in a diary or written on a calendar. So my original idea for this month's poem changed as I was thinking about it.

February

What most people associate with February is St Valentine's Day, but I don't write romantic poetry. It's very difficult to write well and bad romantic poetry is just, well… bad. So I was looking for something connected with relationships which wasn't to do with lovers.

Friendship can be a close tie, and can last even longer than a romantic relationship. I've known my oldest friend almost twice as long as I've been married. It's a very different relationship, not as close as marriage of course, but with a shared experience of early life and school, which makes it important to me.

It's interesting too that, while romantic relationships seem to have changed during history – I'm not talking about emotions, but about what the society of the time 'allowed' – friendships don't seem to have changed character very much at all. Not, that is, until recently.

Nowadays people seem to make friends online as much or more than in real life. I've never really understood this. Maybe it's because I write for a living, but I view any protestations of friendship with deep scepticism if they're made purely through the media. It's all so one-dimensional; the person posting the comments or pictures can say whatever they like and there's no check at all. You can't always get an accurate idea of someone even if you

Opposite page: Fairy house at Milntown, Ramsey
This page: Fairy door in Summerhill Glen, Douglas

meet them, but unless you do meet them, see them, talk to them, you can't even begin to make up your own mind. Online, the only information you have is what they themselves provide, and that might not be true: we've all heard about online grooming, bullying, trolling. Fake friendships are just a lesser aspect of the same thing.

OK, I thought, that gives me an idea. I'll write a poem about what's real and what might not be.

WHAT'S REAL?

Glued to her mobile, fingers flying
She texted, barely heard me, trying
To crop her news to fit her need,
Practice made perfect as she keyed;
Updating, 'liking' this and that
Too occupied to stop and chat.

I pondered changes made by years,
A young girl's dreams, her hopes and fears.
And realised that, in all but name,
Her aspiration's just the same.
Her ancestors believed in elves,
Her gran put milk out for themselves;
The little folk were owed respect
To circumvent their ill effect.

We call things 'accidents' and judge
That's all. We miss the unseen nudge
Of fairy fingers spinning plates
Or taking socks and jamming gates.
Car engines that refuse to start
We don't attribute to their art.
Invisible, they can't exist;
Our modern minds see such dismissed.

Yet though we think them odds and ends,
They're just as real as Facebook 'friends'.

March

I was considering what to submit for March's poem when I heard something which appalled me. The Isle of Man is very fortunate in that it has relatively little crime. That doesn't mean, however, that we don't get some antisocial types who think it funny to cause problems for other people.

A friend of mine, Martin Bosscher, runs a second-hand bookshop in Peel (I spend far too much

Rocky coastline at Port Mooar, Maughold

A ROCKY STORY

My car is old and simple
Just like me (without the dimple)
So I thought it safe to park it on the road.
I went away and left it,
But ended up bereft, it
Being vandalised; the damage clearly showed.

A dirty great big boulder,
Far too large for me to shoulder,
Had been tossed right through the window of my car.
You might think that this sounds funny,
But it cost a lot of money,
And, without transport, I'd not travel very far.

My job is self employment,
So my car's not for enjoyment;
I need it to get stock and get to work.
As I swept up all the debris
I was hardly feeling carefree;
What had I done that some man had gone berserk?

The authorities were friendly
And gathered an assembly
Of forms, reports and – yes – a breakdown van.
The police tried to get going
But no clues left them unknowing;
They admitted that they couldn't catch the man.

My car went to a garage,
The repair bills were quite savage,
I was worried and felt skint I must confess.
The insurance paid at last
(Future premiums will be vast);
Someone's selfishness has cost me time and stress.

The car's now back and mended
But don't think this story's ended.
'Cos it's not while nasty vandals get away.
If you know who did the throwing
Thus described in the foregoing
Please report it, so that we can make them pay!

money in there) and had parked his car in one of the roads near the Manx Museum in Douglas. When he returned to it he found that someone had thrown a very large rock – one he himself could barely lift – through one of his car's windows. The window was shattered of course, and there was glass all over the seats, with the offending rock sitting in the middle of the mess.

Like most of us, Martin gets by, but few of us have huge amounts of spare cash, and he was left with a damaged car, no means of getting to work and an excess bill on his insurance. He was much more sanguine about it than I would have been (and, indeed than I was) and has kept the rock as a souvenir and talking point. When he told me about it, I stomped up and down his shop, gesticulating, and pontificating at length about how awful it was that someone had done this. I think he was amused – by my reaction, not by the incident – and suggested that I write a poem about it. So I did.

Because it was easier, I wrote the poem in the first person as though the incident happened to me. It didn't, but everything else is true. If you want to check it out, the rock now has pride of place in Martin's bookshop at 10 Michael Street, Peel.

April

This was the month that the Manx Bard was involved in controversy!

I firmly believe that, although big, this planet's resources are finite, so we should husband them and use them wisely. Consequently I approve of most things which help to do that. Avoiding waste. Recycling. Mending things, not throwing them away if they get broken. Wearing things out, not just buying new when we feel like it or when fashions change. I also like the idea of renewable energy. But I think we're getting it very wrong.

Wind farms for example. They are excrescences on both land and sea.

I might be prepared tentatively to support them if they worked, but they don't. Not really. The amount of energy needed to make, install and maintain a wind turbine is debatable, as is the amount of energy each will produce over its lifetime. What is reasonably certain is that it takes decades for each turbine to produce the amount of energy expended in making it.

Statistics are available but they are produced either by those in favour of wind turbines, such as manufacturers, or by those very much against them, such as those wedded to more traditional forms of energy production. Consequently such statistics are unreliable, particularly as they often don't factor in things like the energy needed for maintenance and for such maintenance vehicles to get to the wind farm in order to repair it.

We worry – rightly – about polluting our oceans, but I can think of little more polluting than huge artificial spikes driven into the ocean bed disturbing marine life, bringing dangers to flying birds and, possibly being a hazard to shipping. Yes, there are corridors through them, but what about storms? If ships can be driven onto Conister Rock in Douglas Harbour, I think that several hundred wind turbines must pose a bigger danger.

And they look so ugly. No one, as far as I know, took any notice of whether people minded having to live with these ghastly things. Resenting the proliferation of windfarms polluting the Irish Sea I wrote a sonnet about them.

The above text was, to all intents and purposes, what was included in the newspaper. On its publication I was telephoned by a gentleman whom I didn't know, but who was overflowing with approval and relief that someone had actually said what he had been thinking for some time. When I read the poem out during a talk I was giving, again there were a lot of nods among those listening. On the other hand, I was pilloried by the Chairman of the Manx Friends of the Earth who wrote a vitriolic letter to the paper calling me names. The statistics he supplied to support his views were perhaps debatable – see paragraph five above – but I didn't debate them because, rightly or wrongly, I didn't feel that a fanatic was open to rational debate. I also didn't want to drag the post of Manx Bard into disrepute. See what you think.

Seajacks Scylla, windfarm installation vessel, Walney windfarm

SONNET

OFFSHORE WIND FARM

Striding across the sea like Fionn mac Cumhail
These are no mortal, nor immortal things
No giants freed from legend, marked with wings
On their feet. These tridents glitter with jewel-
Bright arms turning lazily – or not. Fool.
Unasked we lacked the smallest inklings
Of their intrusion. Like bad kings
They invade and straits fall beneath their rule.

Tribrachial monopod polluters;
Savage spikes drilling the ocean bed,
Hazard to shipping and horizon looters,
Cluttering litter, profitless and dead
Allowed because the energy is 'clean'.
We believe the lie and then we call it Green.

May

Part of the job of Manx Bard is to talk to individuals and groups about the Isle of Man in general and the Bard in particular. One of these talks was to those living in a care home. It wasn't a big audience, but the elderly residents who had chosen to come and listen to me, were obviously interested and asked a lot of pertinent questions.

Almost all of the audience had some form of mobility difficulty – they used wheelchairs, or walkers or Zimmer frames or the like – but the fact that their bodies were wearing out, didn't mean that their brains were letting them down.

I was reminded quite forcibly of my mother-in-law (see photograph, left), who was an amazing woman and still active and *compos mentis* well into her nineties. Occasionally I gave her a lift to doctor's appointments, opticians and the like and, almost invariably, they treated her as though she were a child. This is a woman who, at 76, decided to learn Portuguese and took an O level in the language, passing with distinction. She was the oldest student in the class by several decades. The officials who spoke to her loudly and slowly all meant to be kind, and often were, but she would frequently say to me that she wished people would look beyond the wrinkles.

My father was another case in point (see photograph opposite). A lovely man, he occasionally gave odd or foolish answers to questions asked him, not because he was stupid or gaga, but because he was deaf. He hadn't heard the question properly and so didn't answer it correctly. ('I'm not wearing those hearing aids; they make me look old.' 'Dad! You're 89!')

Until he retired, Dad was a professional aeronautical engineer who had worked on the undercarriages of both the Harrier jump-jet and Concorde. He wasn't daft. In fact he kept a small plastic bag of glass spheres on the coffee table just so that he could tell various health-care workers that he hadn't lost his marbles.

Old age will happen to most of us, if we're lucky. And, whoever we are, we will probably have to cope with failing health of some sort. With the example of various feisty elderly relatives in my mind, I wrote *Old Age*.

OLD AGE

I've out of date clothing and, which is sadder,
Unrecognised wisdom (plus an impatient bladder).
Forget about knee joints which ache in the rain
And try to remember that I have a brain.
Don't look at the shell, because now it lies,
Don't look at the wrinkles, look at the eyes.

I still have opinions and knowledge and skill.
I still have ambitions I'd like to fulfil.
In my time I've experienced sowing wild oats,
I've partied, got drunk and manned the lifeboats.
I've worked hard and saved hard and earned my pay;
I'm much more than the shadow you see here today.

The current political sphere I abhor,
But no-one asks me what I think any more.
Old age and illness are only a sham;
They say nothing about who I really am.
Don't look at the outside, as that's life's debris,
But find out what's inside, because *that* is me.

June

In many respects, life on the island revolves around TT fortnight. When the season opens, things have to be 'done in time for TT'. Alternatively, work is put off 'until after TT'. Although the races officially last for two weeks, many of the other fifty weeks of the year seem to be taken up with preparation for, or post-mortems after TT. Don't misunderstand; I'm not knocking it. The Tourist Trophy is not only a major spectacle, a revenue generator and great fun, it also makes the Isle of Man famous globally.

I grew up in Cheltenham in Gloucestershire, England. Cheltenham too has a racing festival, but for horses not motorbikes (for a Manx connexion, Trevor Hemmings' Cloudy Dream came third in the Ryanair Chase at the Cheltenham Festival on 15 March 2018). The town is home to the Gold Cup, a premier steeplechase race, and the most prestigious of all National Hunt events. Every year, in March, Cheltenham hosts a friendly invasion, mostly from Ireland. As a teenager I earned holiday money working in the Gloucestershire equivalent of Bushy's Beer Tent. Even the Gold Cup, however, hadn't prepared me for the TT.

Dean Harrison (No. 5) overtaking Conor Cummins (No. 1), between Joey's and the Guthrie Memorial, to be second and third in the Senior Race of the 2018 TT

I well remember seeing the motorcycle race for the first time. It was a lovely sunny day. An elderly lady was weeding her flower beds. Her equally elderly Jack Russell terrier was snoozing on the garden path. No more than twelve feet away, on the other side of her garden wall, motorcycles were roaring down her domestic street at 100+ mph. It was just surreal.

Those taking part are all crackers of course. Brave, certainly, but totally mad. This poem was another one which raised one or two comments. The problem was the final line.

TOURIST TROPHY

The roar of the motor
The tension – he's off!
With support of promoter
And cheering far off.

Down Bray Hill, then hold tight
For Quarterbridge thrills.
At Braddan Bridge, left, right
Speed past Union Mills.

Drop down to Glen Vine
Then Crosby, two Greebas
(Castle then Bridge), no sign
Of the leaders.

Ballacraine, Ballaspur
Laurel Bank, then Glen Helen
Goes past in a blur,
Sarah's Cottage, crowds yelling.

Take Drinkwater's Bend
Handley's Cottage – quite narrow;
Watch the back end –
Speed down Barregarrow.

Cronk Urleigh comes quick
(Careful!), Douglas Road Corner,
Open up through Kirk Mick
No underperformer,

Birkin's Bend at Rhencullen
Bishopscourt, Alpine Cottage
Going well, mustn't pull in
So far there's no stoppage.

Ballaugh Bridge, the bike's flying –
Throttle back, Quarry Bends;
The rider's defying
Lap records and trends.

Sulby Straight, top two hundred,
Brake round Ginger Hall –
Over half way – then thundered
Past 'K', Kerrowmoar.

Glen Duff, then Glentramman
We're now in Lazayre
Milntown; get a scram on
Through Parliament Square.

Through Ramsey, up May Hill
Twist round the Hairpin
All the riders today will
Be out for a win.

The Bends of the Gooseneck
The Guthrie Memorial;
He's giving the low-tech
A TT tutorial.

Mountain Mile to Verandah,
Over Bungalow tracks,
Hailwood Rise understand
There's no time to relax.

Brandywell, Keppel Gate
Famed Kate's Cottage dogleg,
Down the long straight
To the turn at The Creg.

Brandish corner, Hillberry,
Governor's Bridge – don't diminish
The speed, although wary –
Blast through to the finish.

The lap time's a record
Jubilation all round;
The rider aboard
Did the bike makers proud.

He conquered the earth
With thrills, spills and shocks,
But I ask is that worth
Going home in a box?

July

I'm always amazed by how small Tynwald Hill is. For something so historically important, not only to the Isle of Man but democracy generally, the hill is metaphorically enormous. Yet in reality it isn't. It stands quite modestly not far from the A1 in St John's and, if traffic is busy, can even be missed by drivers concentrating on overtaking the bus and avoiding the tractor…

I can think of no other site of such importance which is so self effacing. Stonehenge is smaller than you might expect, but still dominates the landscape for miles. Edinburgh Castle stands proudly on its rock looking down on Scotland's capital. Ireland's Giant's Causeway is a UNESCO World Heritage site. Yet for 364 days of the year Tynwald Hill stands there, quietly, doing what the Manx (and the rest of the British Isles) do best. Not showing off.

Every 5 July, however, or the day nearest to it if 5 July is a Sunday, Tynwald Hill is the focal point for the oldest demonstration of democracy in the world. The customs and procedures of Tynwald have been enacted annually for more than a thousand years, and very few organisations can match that.

The thing I find most impressive about Tynwald, is how little the ceremony has essentially changed. There has been tinkering

---

TYNWALD DAY

For one day in the year this isle forgets
The modern, broadband, space age internets
And looks to one small unassuming mound
Which this day with Manx stateliness is crowned.

Sword of State, procession, pageantry,
Flags, parading VIPs, and dignity:
Another Tynwald Day, just one of many;
An annual celebration – ten a penny.

But old midsummer's day, for eons central
To turning seasons, still is fundamental.
And, stretching back through history's march of time
Machine Age, Tudor, Viking leaders climb
The same hill, at the same time, for the same cause:
To promulgate the island's new Manx laws.

The island parliament, which, on this site
A thousand years or more by Viking rite,
Lets every Manx petition their idea
Of how their land should run from year to year.

The dignitaries in state on Tynwald Hill
Should know they take their seat by common will.
Now elevated they can be displaced
By others who the people's will embraced,
And only those whose fittingness is proven
Should follow in the steps of Godred Crovan.

This tapestry of splendour, this mosaic,
Some label and dismiss as just archaic.
Curious, quaint, unique these rites may be,
But central to the Manx remaining free.

over the years of course, with different officials taking over different parts of the ceremony, but very little has been altered out of recognition. Vikings could turn up in the TARDIS, and instantly understand what's going on – and probably disagree with it. (Vikings loved a quarrel!) One of the earliest records of a Tynwald meeting dates from 1422, and its description could reasonably apply to what happens today. The only significant changes in a modern Tynwald are that women are allowed to take part, and that we use microphones rather than shouting.

I find something very special in tradition. The idea that we do something which has been done by many before us provides a very real link with our history and our ancestors. Tynwald is like that. So I tried to write a poem about it.

August

The Bard's term of office ends at the end of August, so the August poem was my final poem as Manx Bard to appear in the *Manx Independent*. I thought at first about submitting the poem *Farewell*, which appears on page 95, but I wanted that to be fresh for the new Bard's inauguration, and the newspaper appeared a fortnight or so in advance of that. *Spotlight* (see page 26) was also a possibility as no-one had seen it before, but it didn't feel quite right.

Then I thought about how the different bards come to prominence for their year in office, and then recede into the background to leave the next bard space to put his or her stamp on the post. The earlier bards don't disappear completely, however, but are lurking out of sight, if I can put it like that, and appear again from time to time, as required.

I live in Maughold parish, and Maughold mist does something similar. It doesn't appear for days and then, when conditions are right, it floats down over Maughold Head, advancing over the fields and changing the appearance of the landscape. It almost looks like slow-moving water before it retreats to leave everything as it was before. It's quite fascinating to watch.

MAUGHOLD MIST

Shy tendrils reach from port and cove
Venture inland through tree and grove.
Ghostly fingers curl round barns
Throw blankets over roads and farms.
Waves tumble over Maughold Head
Fill cauldron valley, rise and spread
Submerge the lighthouse, church and all
Beneath awhile cocooning pall.
Green turns to white, view loses clarity
And objects lose familiarity.

A pause. Soft undulations these;
Ephemeral, challenged by a breeze.

Waves gently ripple and recede
Objects emerge, but shapes mislead;
Known, but glimpsed through lacy fronds
Are strange until released from bonds.
At length the tendrils flee like smoke:
Manannan dons again his cloak.

The poem was tricky to write as mist by its very nature must be ephemeral. I hoped it might do and was very reassured when I was contacted by a reader of the newspaper who kindly said how much she liked it.

CHAPTER 5

DUTIES AND APPEARANCES

From my point of view it was a rollercoaster of a year. From being appointed and knowing nothing, to a year later and still not knowing very much, I did all sorts of things which I never thought I could. The first thing I was asked to do was to appear with Pullyman and Friends at a poetry event put on in conjunction with the Manx Literary Festival. For readers who don't know, Pullyman, aka Michael Cowin, was diagnosed with Parkinson's Disease in 2006 and has since then raised large sums for the Parkinson's Disease Society on the Isle of Man, often through writing and performing poetry. To put it bluntly, he's a Big Noise.

I hadn't done anything like this since I was at school. Quite apart from the nerves, I didn't want to let anyone down. Fortunately we were allowed to read

Left: detail of embroidery on Manx Bardic robes
Right: Fairy Bridge on A5, south west of Santon

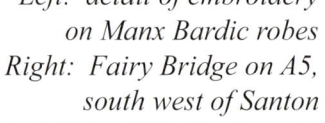

SONNET

ACKNOWLEDGING THEMSELVES

Respected once. Feared, even. Not now. Save
The legend, all else taken from you; wings
Name, even existence. Shady Changelings
Fading into otherness never gave
Proof to mortal belief. We are slave
To what we see. The subtlety of endings
Passes us by. Only your bridge brings
Our tributes now – a giggle and a wave.

But in that hidden unknown realm
Where memories lie abandoned,
And past ages threaten to overwhelm
Our superficiality, we learn, understand and
Look beyond the mocking pantomime:
There you stroll between eternity and time.

our poems, in other words, we weren't asked to recite them from memory. Apart from the fact that the memory works less well as I've got older, I find trying to learn my own poems particularly difficult as I have a tendency to wander down the *cul de sacs* of all the lines I *didn't* use. This might provide the audience with the sort of entertainment they didn't expect but it does wreck the poem.

Those taking part in Pullyman and Friends were asked to do three poems and, in line with my decision to write something new every time I was invited somewhere in my official capacity, I put together *Acknowledging Themselves*, as one of my three. The Manx rarely refer to fairies by name, usually calling them, 'the little folk', 'them that's in', or 'themselves'. As most people know, those crossing a Fairy Bridge should acknowledge the little people with a wave or they will be offended and bring you bad luck.

Poetry readings were one thing, but during the year I also gave a number of talks to different schools and organisations about the Isle of Man and the Manx Bard. In one sense I preferred this as it seemed more likely that I would reach people who wouldn't normally be interested in poetry. It was my job to make sure I didn't put them off completely…

The talks were all loosely based on the same information of course, but I included poetry in each of them and tried to make both the talk and the poems relevant to whatever group I was addressing. I wanted to be sure that someone could listen to me talk more than once and still hear something new. *Top Right-hand Corner* was for the Maughold Social Club, for example, while *After Work*, was for the Manx Retirement

TOP RIGHT-HAND CORNER

Comeovers came to Maughold, found it good;
A place to raise their children, grow their food,
Argue politics and meet their neighbours,
Grow old, have fun when resting from their labours.

Not of today I speak, but long before
Even the Vikings settled on this shore.
An age of stone, which people shaped by hand
Stone still there is, the ribs of Maughold's land.

They're buried here where memories are long
And children's children grow up to be strong,
Knowing their roots and breathing Maughold air.
The ancient crosses raised, now housed with care
The keeills respected, one, now parish church
Still ministers to those in need who search
For spiritual truths. A farming parish
Fields and livestock, no big towns, but lavish
With glens, their waters racing to the sea.
Farm-, fish-, and mining, Maughold has all three,
Hemmed by Barrule, which stands against the sky
From edge to edge, eight miles as ravens fly.

Still people live in Maughold find it good;
A place to raise their children, grow their food,
Argue politics and meet their neighbours,
Join the social club and rest from labours.

Those lucky to live here give silent thanks
That Maughold is just part of being Manx.

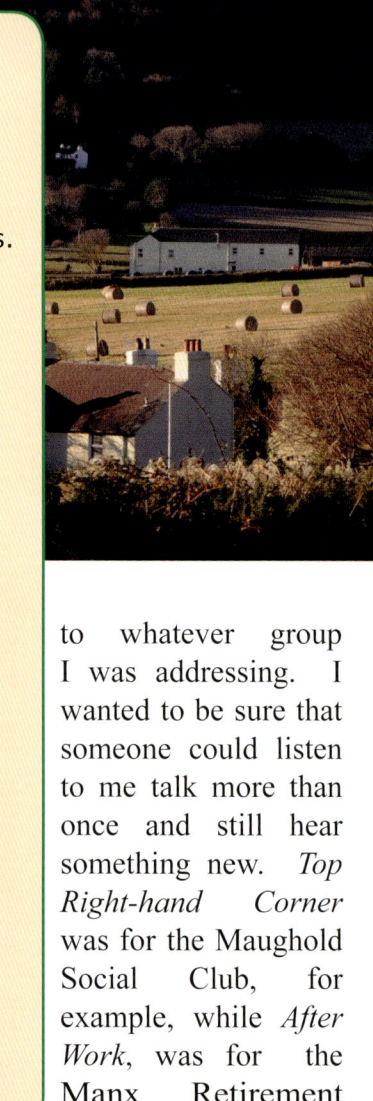

AFTER WORK

My wife is flower arranging,
I've a Russian class at one,
My sister's doing yoga –
She tells me it's great fun.
We try Manx conversation
Every afternoon at three
And every other Tuesday
We go out with friends for tea.
I've rearranged the treasure hunt
For this time Wednesday week,
And we should be going swimming
But the pool has sprung a leak.
We've a tea dance and some cooking
To rival Masterchef,
And trombone for beginners
Who can't recognise a clef.

Next week it's bungee jumping
As long as there's no rain,
And that chap from off the telly's
Going to talk about the brain.
We've passed with flying colours
The university of life.
We're tired of office politics,
Workplace wrangling, and strife.
We don't need a higher income,
And we're fit and in our prime;
We've decided we'll enjoy ourselves
While we still have the time.
We've done our stint of working –
Let the youngsters have a go –
For interest and adventure
Retirement's not for show!

Association. Audience sizes differed tremendously but the best laughed in all the right places, looked interested and asked loads of questions, including the terrible one of 'who is your favourite poet?' I don't know! I like different poets according to what mood I'm in...

There were also seasonal events, three of which I remember in particular. The first was an invitation to take part in a Carol Service just before Christmas at Dhoon Church. Just to be confusing, Dhoon Church is actually in Glen Mona; there are good historical reasons for this which I won't go into here. The foundation stone of the church was laid in June 1854 and it was consecrated in December 1855, i.e. during Advent. I tried to work something of this into *Dhoon Church in Advent*.

The second memorable event was celebrating Burns' Night at Milntown, the stately home just outside Ramsey. Friends had very kindly invited us and, to be on the safe side, I wrote *Burns' Night* in case the organisers might notice

> **BURNS' NIGHT**
>
> You'll notice there's no Chaucer day,
> No Shakespeare celebration.
> No gala for the poet Gay
> For Wordsworth, no libation.
> No 'do' for anniversary
> Of Shelley, Keats or Byron,
> No monies in a bursary
> For doting fans, admiring.
> Though poets such as Donne and Pope
> And Tennyson and Milton
> Of annual tribute have no hope,
> We yearly get our kilt on
> For Burns, young Burns, the Ayrshire Bard
> And noted Ploughman Poet,
> Who made his verse his calling card
> 'Til he had to forgo it.
> Just thirty seven when he died,
> A radical romantic;
> Remembered by the Scots with pride
> His fame is transatlantic.
> His birthday's twenty-fifth of Jan.
> And designated 'Burns' Night',
> With haggis, piping, Auld Lang Syne,
> To celebrated his birthright.
> A toast to Burns: the *only* in
> Fraternity of poets
> Who has a party named for him –
> So raise your glass to show it!

Left: detail of embroidered triquetra on Manx Bardic robes
Right: Christ Church, Dhoon

that the Manx Bard was present and ask me to 'do' something. Just as well: they did! I'm not sure that the hurriedly scribbled verse is the best I've ever done (it isn't), but at least I had something.

I subsequently suggested to the Bardic committee that a Manx 'Brown's Night', with herring and potatoes instead of haggis, should be celebrated every 5 May, the anniversary of the birth of the first Manx Bard, T.E. Brown (see page 12). Watch this space!

DHOON CHURCH IN ADVENT

Consecrated in December,
So Advent was its first event;
For eighteen months each loyal member
Observed Dhoon Church's slow ascent.

Imagine how that congregation
Watched nave and chancel slowly build
Waiting with such expectation
'Til the promise was fulfilled.

Such community rejoicing
Once the waiting time had passed!
Faithful predecessors voicing
That completion's come at last.

Over sixteen decades later,
In church our ancestors designed,
We're here to contemplate a greater
Build up of a different kind.

Advent is a time of waiting
Before the Christmas tale's begun,
Before the party celebrating
Descent to earth of God's own Son.

Advent candles, for Christ's birthday,
Joy and Hope and Peace and Love;
Week by week we light them so they
Turn our thoughts to God above.

Like the Magi, we are travelling;
Gift bearers, not superfluous;
Advent makes us pause, unravelling
The mystery of God's gift to us.

So, celebrate the Christmas season
In due time, but not before.
For the Church year has its reason
And Advent heralds what's in store.

The third seasonal event which particularly stays in the mind was the concert in Maughold church at the end of the flower festival. The festival is island-wide and a large number of parishes took part. The theme was the Manx year.

As the concert occurred right in the middle of the 2018 heatwave I asked if I could change into the robes just before my 'slot'. They're lovely but very warm and I wanted to minimise the length of time I wore them to make sure I didn't keel over in the heat. Not only might that be embarrassing, but a prone Bard would get in the way of the performers. The organisers therefore very kindly allowed me to don the robes in the vestry.

Part way through the concert, therefore, I slipped out of the back of the church, scampered round the outside, passed the door to the loo (as per instructions), and went in through the vestry's outside door. As I donned the robes, I mentally thanked the Maughold sacristan, if there is such a person, for putting a mirror where I could check that the robe wasn't hitched up under one ear (it was), that I hadn't got bits of hair sticking up (I had) and that the hat was on straight (it wasn't). I suppose vicars need to check for similar things before services too. Then I slipped outside again partly to make sure I didn't knock anything over and disturb the performers, and partly to try to find some cooler air.

That's the bit I remember most: waiting by the stonewall of the ancient church (see photograph above), gazing over the quiet graves, while leaning on the Bardic staff and listening to the sweet voices of Marlene Hendy and Dilys Sowrey float through the vestry door. It was incredibly peaceful.

Incidentally, when I wrote *The Manx Year* I didn't realise that *mheileas*, the traditional Manx supper and celebration after bringing in the harvest, *doesn't* rhyme with dahlias. Sorry about that.

THE MANX YEAR

From month to month the rolling seasons frame
The year. Each Christmas sees *Nollick Ghennel*
In lights, on cards; the wish that friends proclaim
To friends. Next day the Hunting of the Wren'll

Bring celebration to Manx streets. Soon, marks
Of planting, shearing in the fields. And lambs.
The tides of visitors and basking sharks
Rise together. Then TT traffic jams.

Racers chase elusive seconds, own
Domestic roads, shave corners, try to cram
More into less. By such speed overthrown
We leave our cars at home and go by tram.

From wheels to feet: in June the Parish Walk
Sees loose-linked chains of people weaving through
Our island, often walking round the clock.
July, a formal, Viking, rendezvous;

Midsummer, when our leaders sit in state
With pomp and fanfare, when old Tynwald Hill
Hosts dignitaries and kings to promulgate
Manx laws, and, by petition, hear our will.

More ancient skills displayed, the Royal Show
Salutes Manx country life, where riding, bees
Cattle, handicrafts, cakes and those who grow
Our food, compete. Soon after: MGP!

Autumn brings shorter days and fruits and grain
Lammastide, well-visiting and *mheileas*,
Leaves falling, swallows going back to Spain,
Flower festivals displaying dahlias.

No Halloween is here; we've Hop tu Naa.
Oldest and unbroken Manx tradition
Welcome and herald to Old New Year's Day
With turnip lanterns, singing and musicians.

The seas grow rough, Manannan rests in dock.
The sea god's fast craft cannot take the strain
Of stormy weather. Farmers bring in stock.
Before you know it, Christmas comes again.

Very much to my surprise and gratification I was also occasionally asked to repeat particular poems which members of the audience had heard me read at different events. One of the most frequently requested was one written about some residents of Dhoon and the people who visited them (see right). It's a mere frippery, but I rather like it. Unlike most of my poems it doesn't have a title.

Right: The beach below Dhoon Glen
Below: Dhoon Glen from the sea

> 'Nice to meet you! Visiting?
> It's a lovely place to be.
> Stroll about, take time away.
> There are lots of things to see.
> The view's tremendous from the cliffs
> – I know places hereabout –
> And the family visits often
> It's a regular day out.
> We like to see the flowers
> And the M.E.R. is fun
> We stroll the fields and footpaths
> And let the kiddies run.
> In fact they're getting older
> Almost ready to leave home;
> I worry they grow bolder
> And go further when they roam.
> Nice to meet you, anyway!
> ... What's that idea you float?
> Will my kids go to college?
> Don't be silly... I'm a goat!'

For those few readers who may not know; there is a large herd of wild goat which roams the Dhoon/Ballaragh/Glen Mona area just north of Laxey. Farmers dislike them 'stealing' the grazing but can do very little to keep them out. Passengers on the Manx Electric Railway (M.E.R.) often see them in the fields, and occasionally on the track. Although nice to see, the goats are becoming rather too numerous and something of a pest as they invade gardens and occasionally houses, eating their way through tasty flowers and home grown vegetables.

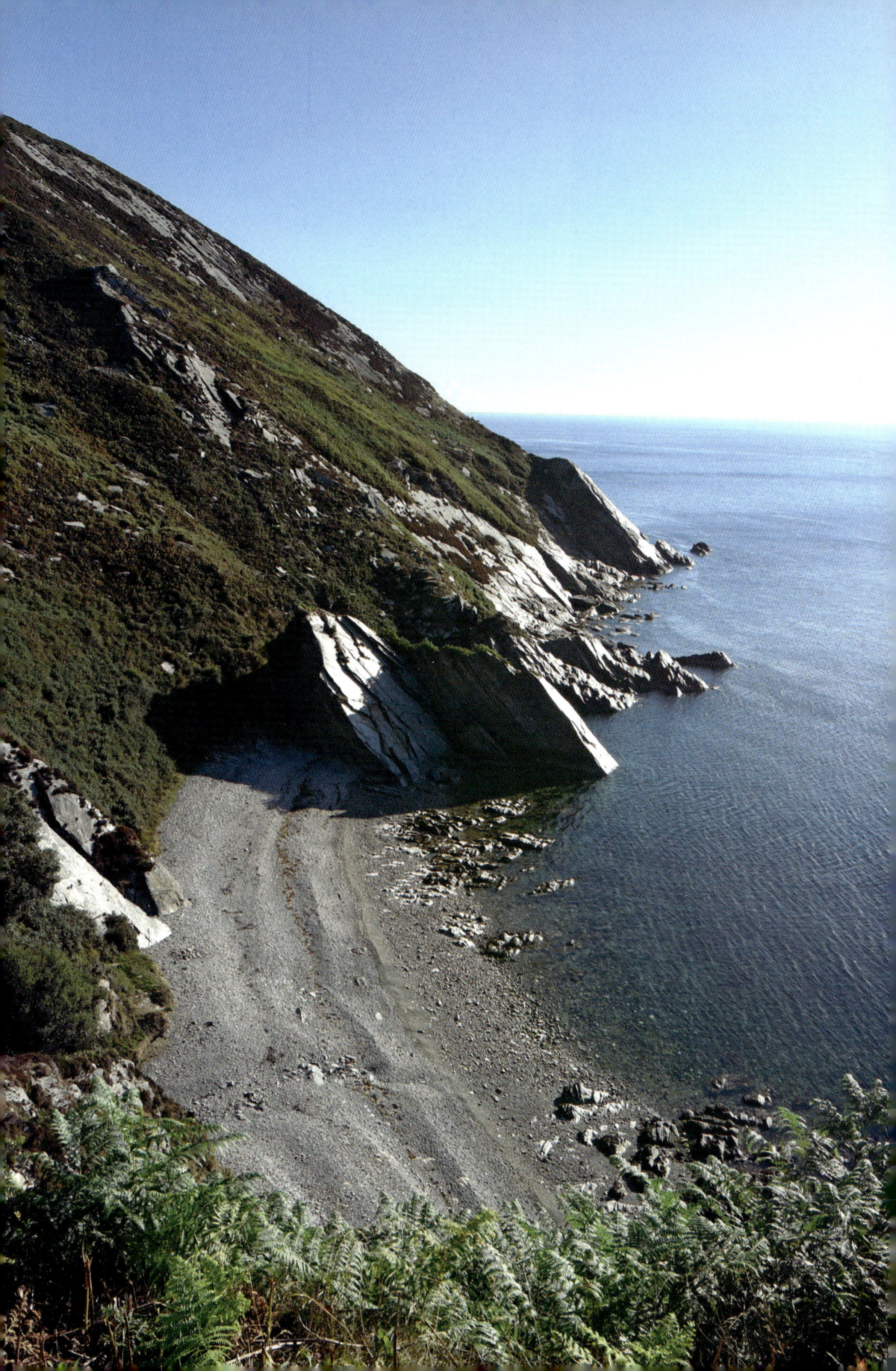

As I've said, the Manx Bard is responsible for deciding how they promote the Isle of Man, and I was keen to take such promotion beyond the island's borders if I could (see next chapter). During my year as Bard, Prince Harry, Duke of Sussex married Meghan Markle in St George's Chapel, Windsor Castle (photograph of Windsor Castle below). The UK's Poet Laureate, Carol Ann Duffy, seemed to be reluctant to do her job of writing poetry to celebrate national occasions, so *The Sunday Times* ran a competition inviting other poets to submit their efforts.

I was alerted to this competition by a friend in the UK, and thought it would be excellent publicity for the Manx Bard if I could possibly win. I didn't win, although I did enter the sonnet *Public and Private*. The

SONNET

PUBLIC AND PRIVATE

The Royal Family – 'The Firm' – recruits
Whom they will. Diplomat or democrat;
Whatever fits the Bill (or Hal) off pat.
Prince and commoner have different attributes
Completing, complementing, rich with fruits.
Harry loves Meghan. She him. So that
'On the stage', 'mixed race', matters not, nor that
The Firm's new member once was star of *Suits*.

Ms Markle's used to cheering and applause,
She'll not be shy of her new royalty,
But, as a princess, within social laws
This former actress will be far less free.
We must support the bride as she begins her
New role in *The Merry Wives of Windsor*.

winner was Graham Wade, from East Yorkshire whose poem begins: 'It is a time of happiness, no doubt,...' Eventually Duffy did write a royal wedding poem, which she sent to *The Guardian* – it seems she was offended by *The Sunday Times* – beginning 'It should be private, the long walk...' I liked his poem, but didn't much like hers. It seems to be a cut-throat business, this writing of poetry.

The new Countess of Sussex's brother-in-law paid a flying visit to the Isle of Man during the 2018 TT festival. Prince William, like his brother, is known to be a motor-cycling enthusiast, although their Dad hates the infernal machines! Prince William might be in direct line to inherit the British throne, but to the Isle of Man, the monarch is the Lord of Man, not the king. I tried to reflect that in *Royal Visit*.

ROYAL VISIT

Among the many visitors who come
To see the Tourist Trophy thrills and spills,
The future Lord of Man makes one
In the crowd.

I wonder if he'd like to have a go
And race his bike through sinuous Manx hills;
Forget the prince and be the man? Even so
It's not allowed.

Instead, the less exciting duty calls:
To raise morale, PR, and, while visiting,
To meet support staff with obscurer roles;
A waiting list.

But Mann has much to please for those more free;
Its landscape, people, culture's interesting.
Time presses now – do come again and see
What you have missed.

During the Bardic year there were failures of course, quite apart from competitive ones. One idea which everyone liked on paper, but which never came to fruition was the idea of the Bard visiting cruise ships anchored in Douglas Bay. The Isle of Man has no deep-water harbour, so passengers on visiting ships usually have to be brought ashore by lighter. Those with mobility difficulties often can't manage to transfer from ship to lighter and back again, and some people just don't bother. It seems such a shame that people go to all that trouble to get here and then don't even set foot on shore.

I had the idea of sending the Bard back in one of the lighters to talk about the Isle of Man to those left behind on the ship. I discussed the idea with the people at Fort Anne who arrange the visits of the cruise ships. Everyone Manx-based seemed to think it an excellent idea and it was proposed to the visiting ships. Rules of the sea mean that the captain has the final say about what happens on board his vessel, however, and the captains didn't like the idea. Pity.

Other failures were less obvious. I contacted the editor of a UK poetry magazine, for example, offering an article on the Manx Bard. Sadly, he wasn't interested. I suggested that Manx poets, which includes the Bards of course, could appear on one of the special stamp collections issued by the Isle of Man Post Office. That, I

Cruise ship Azamara Pursuit *anchored in Douglas Bay*

thought, would get them noticed around the world. Unfortunately there seemed to be little interest in that idea either.

Then there was the Bardic event arranged with the manager of a Manx attraction who left without telling me – and without telling his staff about the event. Fortunately I contacted the venue to ask about last-minute arrangements only to be told that they hadn't a clue what I was talking about. At least I hadn't turned up with robes and staff!

I felt strongly that the Manx Bard should put in an appearance on Tynwald Day, the Isle of Man's national day, but there was a mix-up regarding bookings so Tynwald Day passed with no official Bard presence. I don't expect many people noticed, however, other than me.

And of course there was the routine problem of being an after-dinner speaker to people who had dined well and were therefore nodding off. (Or perhaps I was just boring!)

The differing sizes of audience were interesting too. I talked to groups numbering everything from over three hundred to just four. Oddly, I found the small audiences more difficult to talk to, as they were more intimate and, in the case of the audience of four, felt they all knew far more about what I was talking about than I did (yes, they really did!).

CRUISE SHIP

Like Atlantis, appearing off shore
Mysterious in mist, all the more
For being unheralded and linked
With tidal movement. The schedule inked
But not fast. Floating kingdom complete
Unto itself, brought near to meet
The land. And what land? A series
Of ports, interchangeable queries
Muddling individuality
With their differing locality.

And, ashore, few hours to take in
The country's character, mistaking
Nearness for familiarity
Understanding for proximity.
Visitors, welcomed but not understood,
Cherry-pick venues, yet if they would
Stay longer, locals could teach
Of folklore and customs now out of reach.

But timetables nag and ocean
And lunch beckons. Too soon in motion
Ships leave and head for horizon, steady
In open water, some already
Forgetting the hours spent on this shore.

Come again. Do. We've so much more...

One of the duties of the Manx Bard, of course, is to write poetry just to celebrate and record all that makes the Isle of Man great. People – including me – tended to forget that. I tried to write a poem a week, but found the demands of a full-time job plus all the usual domestic chores meant that I couldn't keep it up. Even so, the demand for new poetry did make me look differently at what was happening on the island around me.

As readers will know by now, I live in Maughold parish, so many of my poems are inspired by that locality. For example, there's a lovely walk from Port Lewaigue along the beach to Ramsey. On the way walkers pass what remains of the wreck of the *Cevic*. If they know where to look, passengers on the Manx Electric Railway can also see something of the remains.

The *Cevic* was a Fleetwood trawler which

SONNET

THE WRECK OF THE CEVIC

Bones, their purpose leached
Into sand, surrounded
By pebbles, rounded
Lie forgotten. Bleached
Like old desires, beached
Ribs, by waves pounded
Their horizon bounded
Still seaward yearned and reached.

Never sentient these bones;
Ship's timbers merely, swamped
By visitors and stones.
Children and gulls prompt
To pick and take. Sad pride
Reduced to plaything for the tide.

ran aground in 1927 near where Ballure Glen meets the beach. The circumstances of the wreck are slightly farcical (for details see Adrian Corkill's excellent book *Shipwrecks of the Isle of Man*) but it is famous for being the first time the sailing/pulling (rowing) Ramsey lifeboat *Matthew Simpson* saved lives, when it rescued the six crew left aboard.

SONNET

DIGGING FOR BAIT ON RAMSEY BEACH

Stretching to the edge of the world
The sea a tassel on the hem;
Flat. The beach shimmering, a gem
Of sunlight in the heat haze, curled
Within the bay, wind's temper furled
To playfulness. A diadem
Of blue, gold, sky, sand, the mayhem
Of tides now only patterns swirled.

Oblivious, men stoop with spades
To dig, marring the pristine surface.
Their headway marked by holes, grenades
Of ugliness, their only purpose
To hunt for bait. Amidst such beauty
They think the worms their only booty.

Above: Ramsey beach looking towards Maughold Head
Below: Detail of fastening for feather on Manx Bard's hat

CHAPTER 6

HIGHLIGHTS

Amid what I might call the routine work of the Manx Bard there were a few events which became particular highlights of the year. To me a highlight is not necessarily something of great importance, although some of the events certainly were. I'm counting as a highlight something which either I'd never done before – which meant that I probably found it quite difficult – or something which I thought encapsulated what the Manx Bard is all about. Some were both.

One such occasion was attending the the first of the Lieutenant Governor's Christmas Receptions with Carols; there were two. The invitation catapulted me into panic mode as the dress code was stated to be 'lounge suit'. Now, confession time; I don't go out much, and I certainly don't go out anywhere 'posh' very much. I might be woefully ignorant, but I had no idea what 'lounge suit' meant for a woman. So I did what most people might do who didn't want to appear a complete

Government House, home of the Isle of Man's Lieutenant Governor

idiot, and turned to the internet to look it up. I was immediately showered with advice that it meant anything from a full ball gown to pyjamas. No help there then.

A friend in London advised a cocktail dress (which is what exactly?), but London events tend to be 'dressier' than those outside London. Eventually I compromised on something floatier and strappier than I'd ever worn before, but which I was relieved to find seemed to fit in.

Arriving was embarrassing. The weather was absolutely foul and the journey from where we live is sixteen miles over country roads, so we'd left loads of time to make sure that traffic and/or floods didn't make us late. Well, there was no traffic, as people were much too sensible to venture out unless they had to. No unpassable floods either. Consequently we were embarrassingly early. We should have been quite happy to sit in the car to wait, but were rescued by an anonymous dark figure under a brolly, gesturing us inside out of the rain. Sploshing after him (my heels were much higher than I was used to, so running became a teetering stagger) we found, once inside, that the hospitable dark figure was the Lieutenant Governor, Sir Richard Gozney. And, of course, we were the first to arrive. Not a great start to drag our host out into the pouring rain. We huddled, dripping, round a spectacular log fire, while His Excellency left to sort out the final arrangements with his staff, and, probably, to dry off.

Once more people arrived, we didn't feel quite so much like sore thumbs, particularly as everyone was very welcoming. The canapés and carol singing – I love carol singing – were great fun too.

As a 'thank you' for the invitation and hospitality, I'd written the sonnet *Reception with Carols* for the occasion so, when we were leaving, I handed it to a member of staff with a request that it be passed to Sir Richard in due course. It wasn't until a couple of days later that I heard that His Excellency had actually read the poem out at the second of his two receptions. That was a huge honour and one I didn't at all expect.

A second great honour was presenting the prizes to the winners of the Easter Festival of Full Length plays. For those of you who don't know, this is an international festival of plays held over Easter week, with a different play each night (see also page 88). Various awards are made, including best male and female actor, best ensemble, etc. I don't envy the official adjudicator as the standard was incredibly high. Forget the Oscars; the Gaiety was the place to be.

I had no input into who won what, which was just as well, but, in addition to presenting the prizes, I was asked to give a short talk on all things bardic as a way of papering over the cracks while the official adjudicator went away and sorted

---

SONNET

RECEPTION WITH CAROLS

Government House, its lights ablaze
Reception rooms displayed *en fête*,
Where strangers murmur *tête-à-tête*
And clutch their drinks and canapés.
Where instant friendliness displays
A wish for frictionless debate,
Country to country, state to state
Midst seasonal communiqués.

'The First Noel' the choir is singing;
We interrupt our earthly network
To wonder if the tale still clinging
To Christmas-time might even yet work.
More sincere, we turn again
To peace on earth, goodwill to men.

out the winners. Otherwise the audience would have been left to stare at an empty stage and twiddle their thumbs for half an hour. The timing was traumatic in itself as I'd prepared a talk of fifteen minutes, as requested, and then was asked to stretch it to twenty-five as the adjudicator needed longer than they'd anticipated. Argh! As a result I was frantically trying to remember all the things I'd cut out, and put them back in again, hopefully in roughly the right place.

I'd never spoken to an audience that large before, and certainly never from the stage of The Gaiety or any other theatre. I've never considered myself a 'performer' in any sense of the word, so it was an incredible feeling to stand on the stage where whole worlds are conjured. Terrifying and amazing in about equal measure.

OPENING NIGHT

The lights go down, expectant crush,
The fidgeting, and then the hush.

The curtains part, and, spotlit there
The actors stand as they prepare
To entertain us with their skill;
Rehearsed, word perfect, dressed to kill.

But entertainment is not all
They have in mind, with us in thrall.
The stage can be both lamp and mirror,
Lighten our mind and bring us nearer
To fundamental truths and free us
To see ourselves as others see us.

It can transport us far away,
Yet comment on the day-to-day,
Worlds of magic, times of joy,
Great sorrow, fear – all these deploy.
Escapist, kitchen sink, romance
Satire, tragedy and dance;
They tread the boards, but we're involved,
Committed 'til the play's resolved.

From amateur to Oscar winner,
From veteran actor to beginner,
Historically they stand apart,
Revealing nature by their art.

Left: Detail of embroidered triqueta with circle, sometimes called the trinity knot or Celtic triangle, on the yoke of the Manx Bard's robes
Overleaf: Interior of the Gaiety Theatre, Douglas. Photograph © The Gaiety Theatre

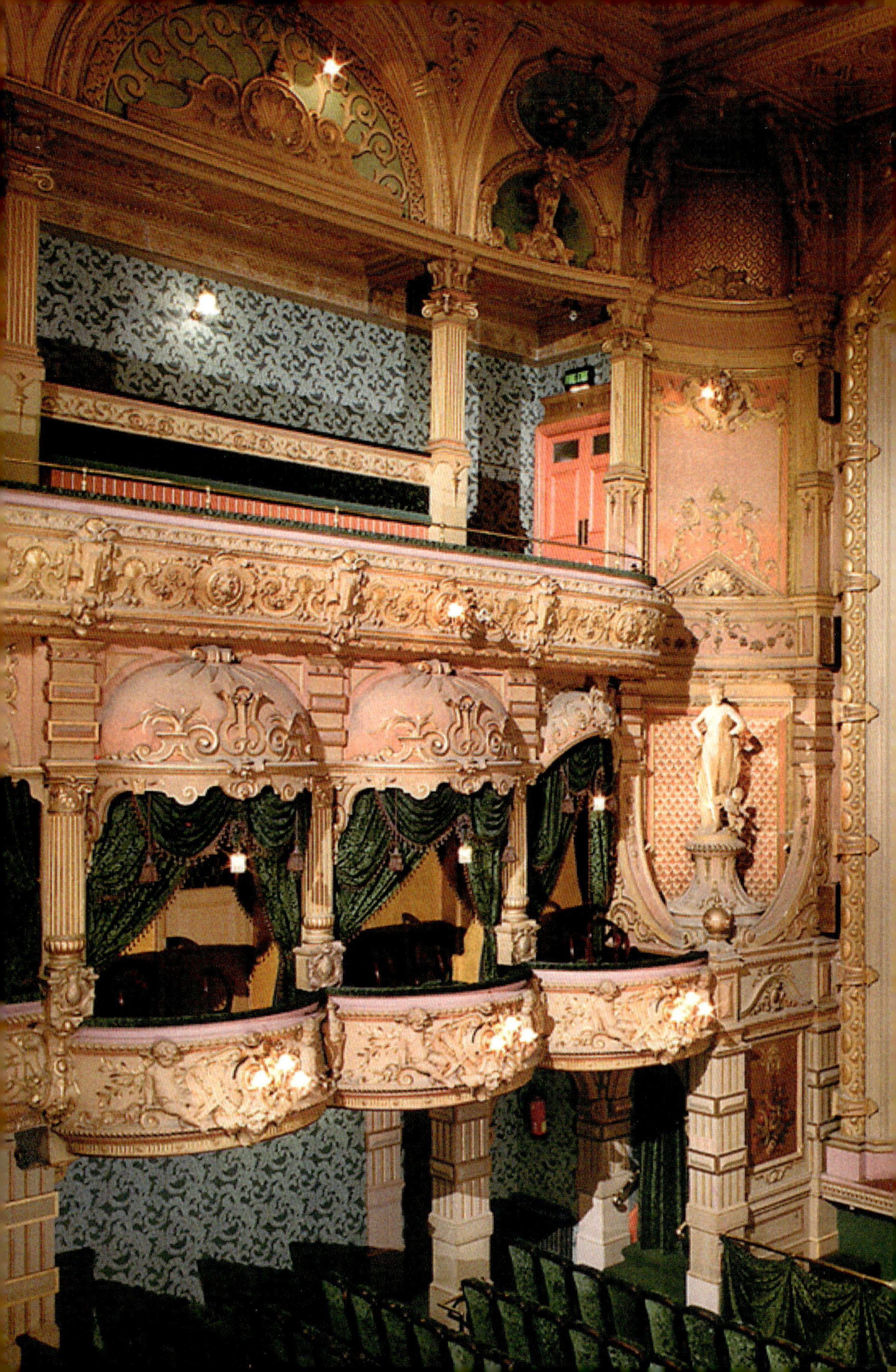

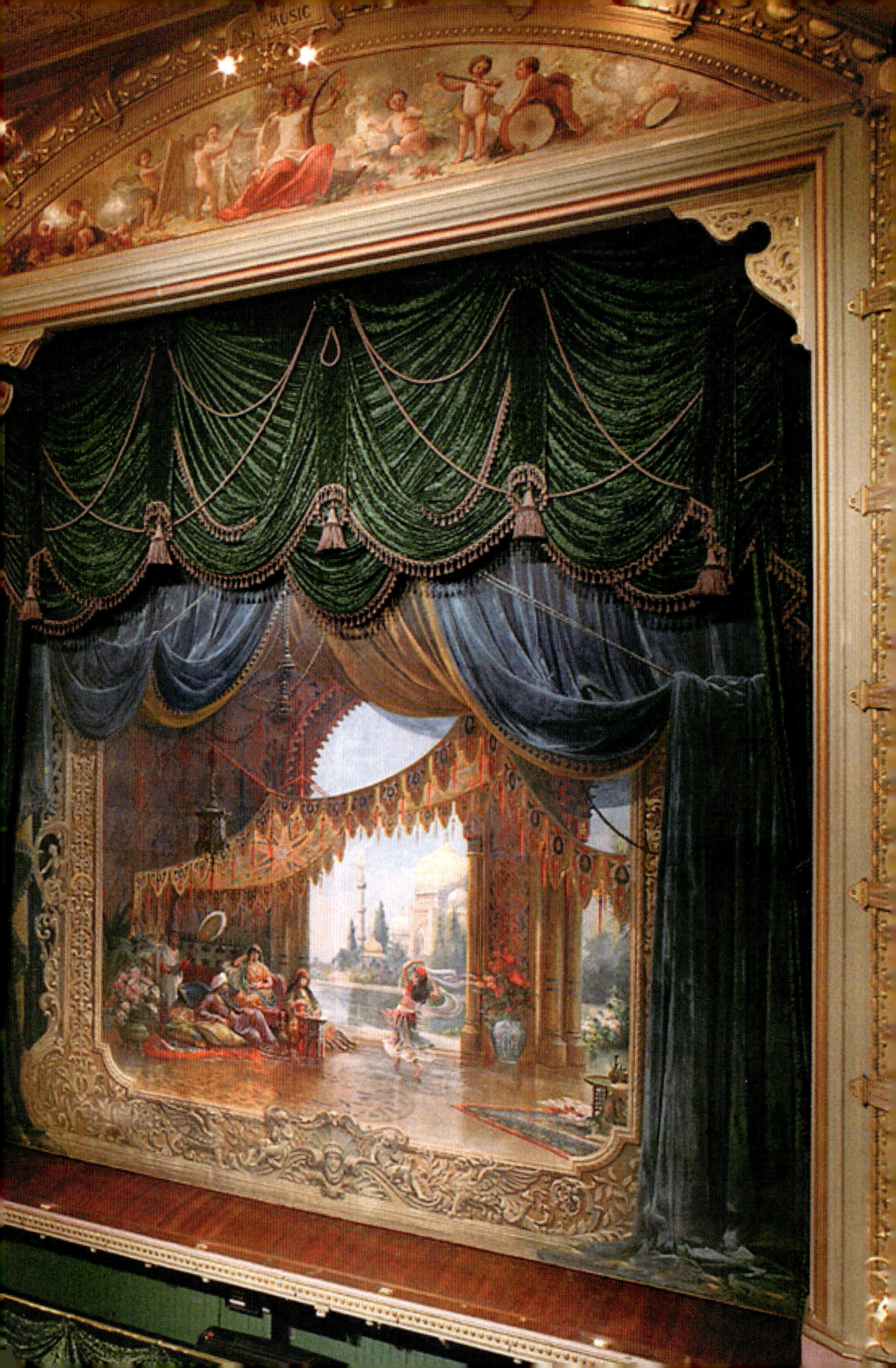
MUSIC

Another prize-giving occasion, this time when I also acted as adjudicator, was for the annual Reading and Reciting Competition at King William's College. The competition was divided into four parts: junior poetry recital, junior reading, intermediate poetry recital, intermediate reading. All the young performers had to do their stuff in front of their parents, peers, teachers, headmaster, and me. I remember, many years ago, I took part in a similar competition when I was at school. I didn't then have any sympathy for the adjudicator. I do now!

The criteria were formidable, including marks for physical presence, voice and articulation, accuracy, whether the speaker was appropriately dramatic and how much they understood of their text. Matthew Taylor, Head of English, kept me on the straight and narrow, and I did eventually sort out four worthy winners. The competition was really close.

The only possible hiccough was, once again, the weather. It was the evening all the snow started; remember the heavy snow in February 2018? I live twenty-five miles from King William's

> **THE MORE THINGS CHANGE THE MORE THEY STAY THE SAME**
>
> I was asked to judge this competition
> To avoid any mistake;
> To concentrate on each rendition
> (Plus I was promised cake).
>
> So I visited King William's
> To discuss the varied clauses
> How to judge the students' brilliance
> In emphasis and... pauses.
>
> We had our consultation
> And agreed in every way,
> But I thought how information
> Had changed since my schoolday.
>
> I learned gallons, feet and ounces,
> Not metres, grams and litres,
> Used log tables, spent sixpences,
> Walked miles not kilometres.
>
> International Baccalaureate
> Was then unprecedented;
> No ICT to glory at –
> Computers weren't invented.
>
> Blackboards, chalk, not screens to touch
> Were how things used to be,
> But, though schools seem to change so much
> They've not, as you will see.
>
> The important things are still the same
> For a rounded education:
> Respect and learning, play the game,
> Discover your vocation.
>
> Academic gifts and sportsmanship
> King Bill's will never lack –
> But it's serious one-upmanship
> To have an airfield at the back.
>
> Each generation thinks itself
> More modern than the last
> But each of us must prove ourself
> Make our future from our past.

College (photograph above), and some of the parents had to come even further. The journey there was fine, but coming back was, er… interesting! Still, it's a boarding school, they have beds; I could have asked them to put me up overnight, I suppose, but I didn't. At times I did wish I had my own snow plough, particularly as I got closer to home. The scenery was gloriously dramatic, but, busy trying to make sure that I didn't slide the car into a ditch, I couldn't really appreciate it.

> Things move on exponentially
> And change is rarely steady,
> Life alters quintessentially
> The trick is to be ready.
>
> One thing I know this college
> And my grammar school both shared
> Is encouraging the knowledge
> That their students be prepared.
>
> So, well done to all who've spoken.
> You've stood and done your best,
> You've kept your nerve unbroken
> And that's the acid test.
>
> The choice has been extremely hard
> Skill shown by everyone
> But now, my duty as Manx Bard,
> Is to announce the four who've won.

As I said above (see page 11) the post of Manx Bard is voluntary and unpaid, so trips overseas to promote the Isle of Man and its Bard have to be done at the individual's expense. I had to go to London on business and so was able to combine it with addressing the London Manx Society (LMS). I'd also promised to bring the Bard's regalia for them to see. However, there was a problem. The robes I could pack, but the Bardic staff was too long to go into my suitcase, and there was no way I was going to entrust it to checked luggage. It would probably have been OK at Ronaldsway, but ensuring it didn't get damaged or 'lost' on its journey through the luggageways of any of the London airports didn't bear thinking about. What to do?

So, I contacted the airline (British Airways) and suggested that it would be excellent publicity for them if they could find a way for me to take the staff with me in the cabin. I didn't expect to be able to tuck it under my seat or in the overhead locker – it's far too long for a start – but thought that one of the cabin crew might put it somewhere safe and hand it back as I left the plane. With some embarrassment, I even offered to travel in the robes if it meant that both BA and the Bard got some publicity. I could envisage pictures of a smiling cabin crew, me in the robes, plane in the background, and the strapline 'BA staff saves Manx Bard's staff', or something similar.

With that in mind I asked the helpdesk, the customer relations people, the press

---

FRIENDS ACROSS THE SEA

The London Manx Society
Avoids all notoriety
But aims, without dubiety,
To promulgate variety
Refrain from impropriety
And say, with due sobriety,
That its members' chief anxiety
Is, publicly and privately,
And short of contrariety
To state, quite undeniably,
Their love of all things Manx.

> **SONNET**
>
> **EXILE**
>
> In Manx descendants, expats, those
> Who simply love the Isle of Man
> Whose life and livelihood is less than
> They would wish, wild yearning grows
> To leave this foreign town, transpose
> Their life to where the fun began
> To Ellan Vannin, where the clan
> Is rocked in Mannin's soft repose.
>
> Support the island, but don't wish
> Your life away. Uprooted, you
> Can stay despondent, moan and languish
> Or adapt in order to be true
> To here and there. Be of good hope
> Life offer's much in her kaleidoscope.

office, the head office and both airports. They all said no.

I pointed out the brownie points they'd get, said they'd done similar things for travelling sportsmen and their equipment, told them about the inestimable help they would be to Manx culture and heritage, and how the Manx people would be forever grateful. Well, OK, that last was a bit of an exaggeration, but I'm sure the Manx press would have included the news.

They said no again.

Well, at least I tried.

Despite being staff-less, the talk went well I thought. Nice crowd, very enthusiastic, asked loads of questions about the Bard, and LOVED the robes – well, who wouldn't! Past President, Alastair Kneale, put me completely to shame as he was a fluent Manx speaker and I shared a table with current president Bryan Corrin and his wife. Membership of the LMS isn't as numerous as it has been – anyone wishing to join would be very welcome (and you don't have to live in London) – but they make up in enthusiasm for the island, what they lack in numbers. And they have the most splendid banner (see opposite page).

If you're wondering why I wrote two poems for the London Manx Society, instead of the more usual one, it's because *Friends across the Sea* was for their magazine. It was only after it had appeared in the magazine that I was invited to be their speaker, so I thought I should attempt something a little less off the cuff, hence *Exile*.

While on the subject of promoting the Manx Bard overseas, it's sometimes said that there are more Manx people living in North America than live on the Isle of Man. I don't know whether that is true or not, but the the North American Manx Association's (NAMA) is certainly a lively organisation.

I contacted NAMA, not with the idea of visiting them (the opportunity would be nice, but cost and time don't allow) but with the aim of asking whether they would include information about the Manx Bard in their newsletter. Kelly McCarthy, NAMA's *Bulletin* editor, welcomed the idea but explained that I'd have to be quick as the press deadline for the *Bulletin* had already passed. It was one occasion when the time difference across the pond worked in my favour: I was putting information together while North America was asleep! As I've always tried to do, I also included a poem. Although *Manx Diaspora* (see page 78) is very short, I was particularly pleased with it, not only because I only had about an hour in which to write it, but because there really was a Kelly in Virginia, a Gawne in Illinois and some Corletts in Colerado.

Another 'first' for me was writing a song – just the words, I hasten to add, not the tune. How it came about is that a member of the audience at one of my talks was Captain Stuart McKenzie, the Project Manager for the Trust which is managing the restoration of Queen's Pier in Ramsey. He asked if the Manx Bard would write a poem about Ramsey Pier in order to help the fund-raising effort. I said I'd be delighted, but after we'd discussed things a little, it became obvious that what he really wanted was a song. I'd never written a song before but I said I'd give it a go.

I have no idea how song-writers usually go about the task

Chief Skedans Mortuary Totem pole, Stanley Park, Vancouver, British Columbia, Canada

MANX DIASPORA

There's a Kelly in Virginia
A Gawne in Illinois
Colerado has some Corletts
Whose life there they enjoy.

What these families have in common
Is their forebears left the fold
To seek new lives across the sea,
But did not forget the old.

Their descendants now live far away
But still give fervent thanks
That wherever they now live and work
They're proud of being Manx.

of writing songs, but it occurred to me that, not being musical enough to write the tune as well, I needed to fit the words to an existing tune, preferably a Manx one. On my way home from that meeting with Captain McKenzie, I found myself humming Harry Wood's tune *The Pride of Port-le-Murra*. The words are written by William Hanby and his chorus starts 'in the land, yes in the land'. I found myself substituting 'Ramsey Pier, oh Ramsey Pier...' and the tune virtually chose itself.

I should perhaps explain that the original song is sung by a gentleman who refers to himself as the pride of Port-le-Murra or, in English, Port St Mary. The modern Manx for Port St Mary is Purt-le-Moirrey, but the title of the tune, as it appears in *The Manx National Song Book, Volume Two*, published by Shearwater Press in 1980, is *The Pride of Port-le-Murra*, which is why I use that spelling.

Port St Mary

Pier of the Realm (see page 80) received its World Premier (that really does have to be in capital letters doesn't it?!) on 13 July 2018 at a concert to raise funds for the Queen's Pier Restoration Trust. It was sung by the Summer Singers, led by Geoff Collier, with Graham Stowell doing a splendid job as the soloist. It was an amazing feeling to hear the verses I'd put together sung by so many people.

One unintentionally funny moment in the concert was caused by the programme. The second item was billed as *Hallelujah*. I'd confidently expected the Hallelujah chorus from Handel's *Messiah*. What we actually got was Leonard Cohen's *Hallelujah*, much, I might say, to my husband's relief. He's not keen on big choral works, but loves Leonard Cohen. I liked it too.

One of the things I've been keen to stress as Manx Bard is that poetry is not 'precious'. Neither is it 'airy-fairy'. To my mind, poetry is one of the most truthful

PIER OF THE REALM

It's the pride of Royal Ramsey.
For the town it is quite handy,
And a marvel of the northern hemisphere:
It's a great historic feature
But the structure has got weaker;
Without help it is about to disappear.

Chorus: Ramsey Pier, oh Ramsey Pier
            You can contribute your pounds and pennies here.
            It's a great historic feature
            But the structure has got weaker;
            Without help it is about to disappear.

So the Queen's Pier Trust was founded
To repair what sea had pounded
With specialists employed to engineer;
They're repairing and replacing
But financial drains are facing –
If you want to help raise funds then volunteer!

Chorus: Ramsey Pier, oh Ramsey Pier
            You can contribute your pounds and pennies here.
            They're repairing and replacing
            But financial drains are facing –
            If you want to help raise funds then volunteer!

We're determined to complete it
And nothing will defeat it.
And, despite what you might elsewhere overhear,
Notwithstanding problems lurking
All together we are working
So Queen's Pier will be again as yesteryear.

Chorus: Ramsey Pier, oh Ramsey Pier
            You can contribute your pounds and pennies here.
            Notwithstanding problems lurking
            All together we are working
            So Queen's Pier will be again as yesteryear.

things you can do. Truthful is not the same as practical, I agree, but there are definite overlaps. All through my year of office I was keen to reach people who wouldn't normally think of themselves as interested in poetry. They might indeed not be, but let's give them a chance to find out. Reading poetry to other poets wasn't really what I thought the Manx Bard should be about.

I was appearing on *Women Today* to talk about the Bard selection process when the main part of the programme was devoted to talking about the current Pension

Matters campaign and the need to make financial arrangements for old age.

Talk about pensions and people start to glaze over, but talk about having enough money to fulfil your dreams and they're more interested. And the two are really the same. If we're lucky we'll get old (I mean that – do you really want to die young?), but that doesn't mean we'll want to stop having fun into our seventies, eighties, nineties. Ever seen a group of elderly people enjoying themselves? They're like teenagers with zimmer frames…

One of the (extremely knowledgeable) speakers was Sharon Sutton, a Chartered Financial Planner, and heavily involved with Pension Matters. She asked if the Manx Bard could come up with a poem they could include on their website and in their documentation. I was delighted to oblige. It seemed to me that this is exactly the sort of thing that the Manx Bard should be doing; getting poetry out there into areas where it's not normally seen. I'm not saying the hastily-written verse was one of my best, because I don't think it is, but if it helps people remember that they ought really do something about arranging a pension, then it's done its job.

PENSION PLANNING

It's right to make provisions
For life in your old age;
Make life-changing decisions
Before you reach the final page.
So, while money's in contention
And the taxman wants more giving,
Do ensure you have a pension
To make sure that life's for living.

CHAPTER 7

PARTICULAR POEMS

During my year in office I've, of course, written a number of poems, usually for a particular occasion or to make a particular point. Several of these I like very much: *Live Interview* (see page 22) for example, and, dare I say it, *Offshore Wind Farm* (see page 43).

There are, however, a number of poems which I wrote simply because I wanted to, or because the poems themselves wanted to be written, and which don't really fit anywhere else. *Legends or Leg-ends?* (see page 14) is one of those, and this chapter contains a few more.

I should perhaps clarify that the first of these, *New Job,* despite the name of the protagonist, has nothing to do with the Parkinson's Disease Society supported by Pullyman (see page 52). It was prompted by friends talking about suffering under poor managers, and my memories of the time before I was self-employed. If there is a problem at work it's usually the administrators and managers who have

NEW JOB

Old Parkinson had worked here
For twenty years or more,
He did his job from year to year
And quietly knew the score.

None thought that we would be bereft
When retirement came to call
And he took pension, clock and left
A Parkinson-shaped hole.

We started distributing
The jobs to get them done,
And HR was recruiting
A younger 'Parkinson'.

The trouble was the new man
Had ideas of his own,
That wasn't part of HR's plan;
What they wanted was a clone.

He believed the bosses' mantra
'Shape the job to suit yourself',
But they didn't want to grant a
Change, and left him on the shelf.

They'd forgotten, when recruiting him,
They'd liked his drive and zest,
His innovations suiting them –
Now he just made them stressed.

They instructed and permitted him
To learn how tasks were done,
But the shape they tried to fit on him
Was the shape of Parkinson.

Days passed, then weeks, and slowly
They knocked his corners off,
They bent, deformed and wholly
Made him see his life's trade-off.

He could have the pay, the pension
As a cushion when he's old,
But must tolerate the tension
And fit Parkinson's old mould.

He went off sick eventually
And, professionally concerned,
They brought in staff potentially
At twice what he had earned.

They claimed that they disliked red tape
And decried their admin roles,
But they never saw they'd often shape
Square pegs to fit round holes.

The author in the Tynwald building, seated on the Bardic chair, with the Manx sword of state in the background. The quotation on the chair is from first Manx Bard T.E. Brown's poem Spes Altera

> **RISK ASSESSMENT**
>
> 'Too risky', they said, 'for him to climb trees.
> 'Too risky', they said, 'for him to skin knees.
> 'No assessment', they said, 'for adventure and sun.
> 'No assessment', they said, 'so it can't be done.
> 'Too risky,' they said, 'for fun'.
>
> 'Too many', they said, 'to come and live here.
> 'Too many', they said, escaping the fear,
> Risking all to flee tyrants, starvation and wars,
> Risking all to flee madmen intent on a cause;
> 'Too many', they said, 'close the doors.'

to sort it out, but if the management is poor then workers have nowhere to turn for help. Bad managers don't recognise that they're bad, or don't care, and have little incentive to correct the problem. This is why so many get away with it and is why it's so difficult to correct.

Risk Assessment is more of a verbal doodle than anything else. It came to me when a group of us had been discussing the ridiculous lengths taken by health and safety measures to protect children nowadays. Then, on the television news, I saw the real dangers faced by boatloads of child migrants. The juxtaposition struck me as grimly absurd.

83

But Bards are supposed to be entertainers too, so, needing something a bit lighter I put together *Procrastination*. Someone did suggest that I call it 'Traa dy liooar', but I resisted. To me the Manx for 'plenty of time' is a much more friendly concept than the postponement suggested by 'procrastination'. And, silly though I recognise it to be, I can't help being frightened by spiders.

PROCRASTINATION

There's a spider in the bath.
Now, you really shouldn't laugh;
It's big and black and hairy in my space.
It's sitting there and glaring
While I'm standing here and staring
With a look of abject horror on my face.

You see, I don't expect it,
And I'm frightened to eject it –
It's bad enough when it is sitting still.
But when those legs begin to scurry
It really makes me worry
And a trickle down the spine gives me a chill.

I could wash it down the plughole
But I'd get a bended lughole
From those people at the RSPCA.
It's not a fair encounter
As it means I must surmount a
Problem when I'm running late today.

So I leave it in possession,
Looking at me with aggression,
But I know I'll have to come back in the end.
I go back to check much later,
Wishing I'd a mediator,
And see to my dismay, IT'S BROUGHT A FRIEND.

Now TWO spiders in the bath –
An appalling aftermath –
Mean the moral of these lines is clear to say:
When irritations bring you sorrow
Don't put off until tomorrow
What you know you really should
      have done today.

Rightly understood, *Learning Manx* (right) is an undercurrent of my entire Bardic year. When I was interviewed for the post of Manx Bard, I had mentioned that I thought it important that the Manx Bard should speak Manx, but that unfortunately I

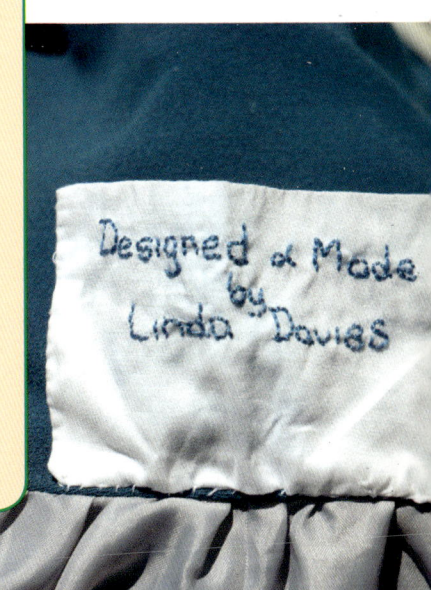

LEARNING MANX

My Manx is fairly undistinguished
(Non-existent's more correct)
I realise, sadly, I'm no linguist;
My mistakes will go unchecked.

Of course I've words like
    traa dy liooar,
Kys t'ou and *kanys ta shiu*,
The first of which means 'time galore'
The other two, 'how are you'.

I even know a phrase or three
In Manx, like *goll as gaccan*,
But 'going grumbling' sounds to me
Like little more than jargon.

And fluency leaves me nonplussed
However I propound it;
Manx defeats me and I just
Can't get my head around it.

For, unlike French or German, say,
When cases need declining,
There, ends of words might go
    astray –
Manx differs in defining.

In Manx you change the letters which
Appear at words' beginnings.
The term's 'lenition', and the switch
Gives Manx its underpinnings.

This means, say, M becomes a V
Just as in *Ellan Vannin*.
Such mutation is the key
To what the word began in.

(The difficulties detailed thus
Just female nouns assail:
Which goes to prove the female is
More deadly than the male.)

Imperatives are hard to learn
Some change quite radically.
In English 'go' and 'Go!' don't turn;
Manx *goll* becomes *immee*.

Manx counting also is possessed
Of difficulties aplenty;
The larger numbers are expressed
As multiples of twenty.

Pronunciation's worst of all
And seems divorced from spelling;
I just don't get the protocol
The word shapes aren't compelling.

I flounder on – but quite right too –
Manx is our country's tongue,
But I wish that what I try to do
Didn't always go so wrong.

But, though I'm poor at languages
It's really no excuse
Manx has diverse advantages
Even though it is abstruse.

Through Manx we can connect
    our lives
With what has gone before;
Our island way of life survives
In language and folklore.

It's right that Manx be taught in
    schools
It's important that it thrive;
A vital one of many tools
To keep Manx heritage alive.

did not. I was attempting to learn but was making a complete dog's dinner of it and not being very successful.

After I was appointed fourth Manx Bard, Phil Gawne, one of the interview panel and a fluent Manx speaker, suggested that I should set myself the challenge of writing a poem in Manx by the end of my year's tenure. I thought this a very good idea but knew that I didn't have a hope of being able to comply with it.

I've never really had the mental agility for sorting out cases, tenses and the like with the speed necessary to speak a language rather than read it, and, with age, seem to have lost the facility for remembering vocabulary easily. I am, however, very interested in linguistics and etymology and have had work, in the past, translating German text into English. Consequently I find Manx fascinating and frustrating in almost equal measures. *Learning Manx* was the best I could do to rise to Phil's challenge.

Harry Kelly's cottage (with fishing net), Cregneash.
Mr Kelly was the last person to speak Manx alone

CHAPTER 8

A LITTLE BIT ABOUT POETRY

If you're not really interested in how poems are bolted together then you probably don't need to read this chapter. They work just as well (or not) even if you don't know what goes on behind the scenes as it were. If, on the other hand, you would like to know a little more about a few verse forms, then read on.

Edgar Allen Poe said that he would 'define the poetry of words as the rhythmic creation of beauty.' Whether you agree with him or not, it's rhythm and not rhyme which defines traditional Western poetry. Neither classical poetry nor Norse sagas usually rhymed, and such poems wouldn't even be written as we do now, with line breaks making up a verse form. To save space, poetry, if it were written down at all and not merely remembered, would normally have been written out as a single block of text. Readers would only recognise such text as poetry by its metre and occasionally by its use of alliteration.

Rhyme seems to have been introduced into poetry from different sources depending on the language in which the poem is written. Poetry in Manx probably began to use rhyme around the sixth or seventh centuries, as the concept was introduced from Ireland: Irish Gaelic is closely related to Manx, there were social and trading connexions between the two countries, and Mann was probably under the rule of the High King of Ireland at the time. Poetry in English first began to use rhyme at roughly the same time, but, probably due to the spice trade, was influenced by Arabic poetry and songs which were intricately rhymed.

Poetry composed by the original bards therefore (see chapter 1) would have had a recognisable rhythm and possibly, although not necessarily, may also have rhymed. For practical reasons alone, metrical rhyming verse is easier to remember, and most bardic poetry would not have been written down.

I hope I don't upset any fellow poets when I admit that I struggle to appreciate free verse, i.e. poetry with no rhyme or rhythm. Robert Frost likened writing free verse to 'playing tennis with the net down', and I tend to agree. I find that the discipline of having to fit within a verse form actually helps me to write better poetry, as it forces me to discover ways of saying things which I otherwise would not. Perhaps I'm merely lazy.

Rhyme schemes in poetry are usually described using the alphabet where the same letters indicate rhyming lines. A poem whose rhyme scheme can be described as AABBCC, for example, is written in rhyming couplets; the first two lines rhyme with each other, the third and fourth lines rhyme with each other and so on. Metre is complicated and almost impossible to describe briefly so I'm not going to try here. Suffice it to say that poetry is made up of stressed and unstressed syllables in different patterns and rhythms.

Most poets, including me, often make up their own verse forms to fit whatever they're going to say. *Royal Visit* (see page 63) with its rhyme scheme ABAC DBDC is one of the more unusual ones I've come up with. Most often, however, I either write in rhyming couplets, or use a recognised and recognisable verse form.

> We're looking to find the next Bard;
> No poets are ever disbarred.
>   If you can write verse
>   Rhyme – or the reverse –
> Have a go, you might have the trump card.

One of the easiest verse forms for anyone to recognise is the Limerick, although no-one seems to know why it's named after the Irish town. It's officially described as an anapaestic trimetre with the rhyme scheme AABBA, but never mind the technical name, almost everyone knows how it goes. One of the things the traditional wandering Bards would be expected to do was to make up rhymes about their present company, which could be rude if they didn't think their patron was paying them enough. While I didn't want to indulge in rhyming rudeness, I did try to use Limericks as a handy way to refer to people by name during talks, or for memorable publicity purposes.

One of my duties as modern Bard

The stage door behind the Gaiety Theatre, Douglas

> The stagemanager's name's Daniel Hall -
> He's in charge of this week's free for all.
>   Here at the Gaiety
>   He's a thespian deity;
> The Manx answer to Sir Peter Hall.

> The Manx Bard Blog is rather belated
> I was told it was time to create it
> I wasn't sure why
> But they said, with a sigh,
> 'To keep interested persons updated.'

was to contribute to the online Bard Blog. I'm not a fan of social media (see *Social Media* on page 94), and am also something of a technoklutz, so my contributions to the Bard Facebook page were sent to the Bard committee who then posted them. As Bard I was supposed to be producing poetry so wanted to include some sort of verse with each blog update. I used Limericks sometimes but also turned to a short Japanese verse form, the Hai Ku, because it was precisely that: short.

The Japanese language doesn't lend itself to rhyming verse, and Japanese poetry relies on counting syllables. Hai Ku have three lines of five, seven and five syllables respectively. The first two lines ask a question which the third should answer.

> Why are Limericks not like Hai Ku
> Three lines each and five, seven, five too
> You can Hai Ku with ease
> If you speak Japanese
> But a Limerick's much harder to do.

Having done one or two Hai Ku for the Bard Blog I thought I ought to mark the new year with a new verse form. Again I was looking for something relatively short and quick as it was a busy time of year. The word *tanka* came up as the answer to a crossword clue and, looking it up, I found that a Tanka is another Japanese verse form, this time with five lines, the number of syllables in consecutive lines being five, seven, five, seven and seven. As it is traditionally used to write about the seasons, it seemed appropriate for a poem about the new year, so I had a go.

> Why are all Hai Ku
> Five, seven and five, metre?
> There are better ones.

> We fly to elsewhere
> Seeking novelty and change;
> Find only ourselves.

I quite liked the result (see *New Year 2018,* page 90) but

must confess to being slightly uneasy about using a verse form designed for a language other than the one in which the poem is written. The slight artificiality imposed on the writing by the structure, it seems to me, can make the poetry appear profound when it's actually nothing of the sort.

NEW YEAR 2018

Sunday to Monday
Ending turns to beginning
Late becomes early.

We watch the new year dawning
Bringing hope on quiet wings.

Beech trees on the B22 at Injebreck, near Baldwin

In our garden we have a magnificent hawthorn tree (see right), or May tree as it's known where I come from. It's a tree traditionally thought to guard the gate to the kingdom of the little people, and, famously, the Glastonbury thorn was supposed to have grown from the staff of Joseph of Arimathea when he visited England carrying the Holy Grail (just go with the flow...). A neighbour, Keith Kerruish, particularly admired our tree, saying that he thought it must be carrying a million blossoms, and asked whether I could write an ode to the hawthorn.

Essentially an ode is a poem addressed to a person or object in order to praise it. Odes are tricky. In fact classical odes are a nightmare to write as they have such an elaborate structure. English odes are simpler, usually but not necessarily relying on the rhyme scheme ABABCDECDE. Probably the most famous ode in English does not use that rhyme scheme at all. *Ode of Remembrance* is verse four of *For the Fallen* and begins: 'They shall grow not old, as we that are left grow old...'

I'd never written an ode before, but I had a go. I must confess to not being totally happy with the result, but then I'm not comfortable with addressing praises to an inanimate object.

Incidentally, Keith very kindly sent *Ode to a Hawthorn* to *Country Life* with the suggestion that they publish it. More publicity for the Isle of Man! Unfortunately they didn't. Sigh.

ODE TO A HAWTHORN

Stately matriarch standing sentinel
Over rumoured portals to fairy realms,
Your branches dipping in intentional
Curtsey; weighted blossom which overwhelms
Our senses. Lacy petticoats, this tree
Wears a million flowers, their scent blowing
Like sweet music in tune with its display.
Sister to Joseph's staff, sense and history
Lead us to admire and, overflowing
With praise, to crown you Queen of the May.

Finally, as readers of earlier pages will have noticed, I do like sonnets. Short poems of fourteen lines in length, sonnets were invented in Italy in the fourteenth century; their name comes from the Italian *sonetto* meaning 'a little song'. There are two main types of sonnet, the Petrarchian and the Shakespearean (there are others) which are distinguished by their differing rhyme scheme. I prefer the Petrarchian, the older form, whose rhyme scheme is ABBAABBA CDCDEE (or occasionally CDECDE). Just as in the question/answer structure of a Hai Ku, the first eight lines of a sonnet pose a question which the final six answer. I find sonnets difficult to write but tend to do so when I have something I think is important to say.

Me, reciting at the inauguration of the the fifth Manx Bard, Annie Kissack

SONNET

RHYME AND REASON

What really is the point of poetry?
Is it mere cant to make our words sound sweeter
With dactyl, anapaest and other metre?
Where counting feet becomes a recipe
To write by rote. When verse-form easily
Assumes importance, meanings teeter
And rhyme and rhythm merely make it neater.
Is the framework really all? I disagree.

I think a poem's far more fundamental.
Its structure frees not stifles meaning.
Its ends – if any – not accidental
But forensically examining and gleaning
Understanding; its conclusions real,
Not things and words, but what we feel.

CHAPTER 9

ME

The Manx Bard is an important role, but is quite separate from the particular poet doing the job for that year. I feel quite strongly that it's the work, and not the identity of the person wearing the robes, which is important, so I was reluctant to include details about me in this book about the Bard's year. I thought such details irrelevant, and probably uninteresting. Various friends and relations intervened however and I have been overruled. So... here goes.

Despite the poem on page 12, I certainly wasn't born to be Bard. I was born in Gloucestershire, England, in a small village called Up Hatherley, now subsumed into a suburb of Cheltenham. About its only claim to fame is that it's near the annual and manic cheese rolling event held at Cooper's Hill just up the road.

I lived in Gloucestershire until my marriage, which began something of a perambulation as we moved according to where my husband's job was. George is a chartered engineer with a PhD, and has worked on a number of high-profile projects, including various oil rigs, the Taiwan high-speed railway, the Dash 8 aircraft, and London Underground. He is very much in demand as a world expert, so we moved a lot. As I am a self-employed writer, I could work anywhere with internet access, a phone and a postbox, so I could take my job with me. This, incidentally, explains why I retained my maiden name, Goodwins, rather than take George's name of Hobbs. Changing both my name *and* my address meant that my customers would not be able to find me, or, if they did, would no longer recognise that I was still me!

Gloucestershire is just about as far away from the sea as you can get in Britain, which is probably why I've always loved the ocean. With my parents and later as an adult I'd always holidayed by the sea and, one year, I came to the Isle of Man. I loved it. When George and I got together I dragged him to the island – as he's a transport enthusiast and already wanted to visit the island's heritage railways this wasn't difficult – and he was similarly smitten. This was the place we wanted to live, although it took several dozen holidays and another twenty years to achieve it.

> **SONNET**
>
> **SOCIAL MEDIA**
>
> Why this sudden mania for media –
> Social lovers, tech or otherwise?
> Are we now no longer motherwise
> Sans wiki- or encyclopaedia?
> Doesn't life become much seedier
> When we and Twitter in the guise
> Of helpful aids tell us official lies?
> While online shopping makes us greedier.
>
> Not for me the prurience of Facebook.
> Denuding self in the bright light
> Of strangers stares who take a look
> Between stations, on the run and a tight
> Schedule. So many peering and staring.
> I prefer privacy, it's less wearing.

Then retirement began to loom for George. He'd always been a keen semi-professional photographer, so with his photography and my writing we decided to start our own publishing house and Loaghtan Books was born. It was UK-based for a couple of years and then relocated to the Isle of Man, and us with it. We'd finally arrived.

I mentioned that I was a self-employed writer and so I am. I've written over a thousand articles for the national and international press, put together non-fiction books on all sorts of subjects and have even ghost-written an autobiography for one of the TV chefs. My liking for words came from my father, who was a lovely man; I was very fond of him. He certainly gave me my love of poetry, although he would have called them 'rhymes'. There's a picture of him on page 45, taken sneakily as he hated being photographed. Remember I said we used to go on holiday to the seaside and that Gloucestershire was a long way from the sea? Well, Dad used to make up rhymes on long journeys to keep us amused. Often they were nonsense rhymes and usually funny. Over the years I gradually joined in suggesting rhymes, and segued into writing some of the verses myself.

Although clever, Dad wasn't particularly well educated, and knew that he often lacked the right word to describe whatever it was he wanted to say. He collected words and often deliberately used them in what he knew were completely inappropriate circumstances just so that he wouldn't forget them. One of my favourites was 'there's a lot of hubris all over the road'. Lovely way to describe self importance!

Dad died.

It was two years ago now and I still catch myself thinking 'I must tell Dad that.' But of course I can't. And I won't ever be able to again.

Rather than just wallow in self pity – Mum had died two years previously after a long series of illnesses which included dementia – I wanted get out of my rut and do something which might have made Dad proud. So I applied to be Bard.

In my mind, merely *applying* was enought to de-rut me, as anything approaching performance was far beyond everything I'd done before. I never in my wildest imaginings thought I'd be appointed (see page 20). George hit the nail on the head when he said that my father would have been really proud, but that he would not have understood it at all. Incidentally, I've been very, very lucky in my life that my two 'main men' have both been extremely lovely people.

A quick word to finish. As I said at the beginning of the chapter, I feel rather ambivalent about any undue importance which is accorded to the writer of poetry – or indeed any other written work. I feel, really quite strongly, that the writer doesn't really matter. It's the writing which matters, and therefore too much stress on the writer is actually wrong. It's a little like having children. You bring them into the world, make sure they have everything they need, and then usher them out to venture on their own. I feel that any form of writing is like that. It should stand on its own (metrical!) feet. I hope that all future Bards have as much or more fun than I have had, and that they pass the staff and robes on without regret.

FAREWELL

Another Bard, of Avon, once
Said 'All the world's a stage',
But when we, each of us, confronts
Our end... our final page,

We should look back at what we've done,
Judge what we have achieved.
For even though our race is run
We shouldn't feel bereaved.

For us the lights may now have dimmed,
But we have walked with giants;
Our efforts here have been untrimmed –
Forget the rest is silence.

Another voice will take the part
And give it their own spin;
New style, new verse, a brand new start:
Let the next Bard now begin!

INDEX OF POEMS

A Rocky Story	40	Offshore Wind Farm	43
Acknowledging Themselves	52	Old Age	45
After Work	55	Opening Night	71
Bardic Botherings	18	Pension Planning	81
Born to be Bard	12	Pier of the Realm	80
Burn's Night	56	Procrastination	84
Celtic Artwork	11	Public and Private	62
Christmas midwife	35	Reception with Carols	70
Cruise ship	65	Return of the Hero	15
Dhoon Church in Advent	57	Rhyme and Reason	92
Digging for Bait on Ramsey beach	68	Risk Assessment	83
Douglas Sentinel	33	Royal Visit	63
…For Mandate interview	23	Ships that pass	30
For Shiaght Laa	26	Social Media	94
Exile	77	Spotlight	26
Farewell	95	Stepping Up	29
Friends across the Sea	76	Thank you	21
Learning Manx	85	The Horse's reply	17
Legends or Leg-ends?	14	The Manx Year	59
Life's Measure	9	The more things change	
Live Interview	22	the more they stay the same	74
Manx Diaspora	78	The Wreck of the Cevic	66
Maughold Mist	51	Top Right-hand Corner	54
New job	82	Tourist Trophy	47
New year	36	Tynwald Day	48
New Year 2018	90	What's Real?	39
Not sure	24	Written by Candlelight during a Power Cut	6
Ode to a Hawthorn	91		

ACKNOWLEDGEMENTS

I am indebted to several organisations and individuals who gave up their time to provide help, information and/or photographic material. They include, individuals: Andrew Barnett, Bob Carswell, Bridge Carter, Hannah Carter, Beth Espey, Sir Richard Gozney, Seamus Shea, and organisations: The Gaiety Theatre, Manx Radio.

Always of course I am grateful for the support and photographic expertise of my husband, George Hobbs.

Thank you all for your help and assistance; any mistakes are entirely mine.